BETTER THAN A LEM⊗NADE STAND!

SMALL BUSINESS IDEAS FOR Kids

WRITTEN BY
DARYL BERNSTEIN

ILLUSTRATIONS BY ROB HUSBERG

ALADDIN
New York London Toronto Sydney New Delhi

BEYOND WORDS
Hillsboro, Oregon

For David and Bianca, who have advised and supported me through each of my ventures; and Siena and Sage, who inspire me every day.

ALADDIN
An imprint of Simon & Schuster
Children's Publishing Division
1230 Avenue of the Americas
New York, NY 10020

BEYOND WORDS
20827 N.W. Cornell Road, Suite 500
Hillsboro, Oregon 97124-9808
503-531-8700 / 503-531-8773 fax
www.beyondword.com

This Aladdin/Beyond Words edition May 2012

Text copyright © 1992, 2012 by Daryl Bernstein
Illustrations copyright © 1992, 2012 by Beyond Words Publishing, Inc., and Daryl Bernstein

For information about special discounts for bulk purchases, please contact Simon & Schuster Special Sales at 1-866-506-1949 or business@simonandschuster.com.

The Simon & Schuster Speakers Bureau can bring authors to your live event. For more information or to book an event contact the Simon & Schuster Speakers Bureau at 1-866-248-3049 or visit our website at www.simonspeakers.com.

Managing Editor: Lindsay S. Brown
Design: Sara E. Blum
Illustrator: Rob Husberg
The text of this book was set in Bembo.

Manufactured in the United States of America 0312 FFG

10 9 8 7 6 5 4 3 2 1

Library of Congress Cataloging-in-Publication Data
Bernstein, Daryl.
    Better than a lemonade stand / Daryl Bernstein. — 1st Simon Pulse/Beyond Words pbk. ed.
        p.   cm.
    "New Edition"—Pref.
    Rev. ed. of: Better than a lemonade stand! : small business ideas for kids. c1992.
    Includes bibliographical references.
    1. Small business—Management—Juvenile literature.   2. New business enterprises—
        Management—Juvenile literature.   3. Entrepreneurship—Juvenile literature.   I. Title.
    HD62.7.B414   2012
    650.1'2—dc23
                                                                            2011033780

ISBN 978-1-58270-330-5 (pbk)
ISBN 978-1-58270-360-2 (hc)
ISBN 978-1-4422-4970-1 (eBook)

Contents

BUSINESS IDEAS FOR Kids

Contents

Preface

At age fifteen, I wrote *Better Than a Lemonade Stand!* because I wanted to share a secret. I had discovered that starting a business was the most exciting, challenging, and rewarding activity I had ever encountered. My goal was to let other kids know that entrepreneurship is the ultimate adventure, and there is no reason to wait until you are an adult to start experiencing it.

This book fulfilled my original goal of sharing my secret, and so much more. *Better Than a Lemonade Stand!* began a youth-entrepreneur movement and inspired a generation to launch its own small businesses. Newspapers, magazines, TV, and radio helped spread the message all over the world. Schools added this book to reading lists and even developed entrepreneurship lessons around it.

Since the first edition was published, I've received more letters and emails than I can count from kids who have started businesses based on the ideas they read about in *Better Than a Lemonade Stand!* Many of these kids are thrilled that their work has produced real income, and others are grateful to learn about entrepreneurship and are looking forward to sharpening their skills.

Being a kid entrepreneur has actually gotten easier since I first wrote this book. Technology such as the internet provides a host of new opportunities for young people with great ideas. Websites provide free education and discussion forums for entrepreneurs, and you can promote your business through social media and other online venues.

You might be interested to know that kid businesses can turn into really big companies. One business I started when I was twelve grew and grew and grew to over one hundred employees! Since I wrote this book when I was fifteen, I've followed my own advice. I took everything I learned as a kid entrepreneur and became a successful adult entrepreneur. Here's the best part of all this: if you start now, you can be more successful than I am!

This is a great time for you to become a kid entrepreneur. Launching your own business will teach you creativity, confidence, determination, flexibility, and the power of persuasion—skills that will serve you well your whole life. Once you learn that you have the ability to turn your knowledge and work into income, you'll be in control of your own destiny.

Wishing you a fulfilling adventure,

Daryl, 20 years older

Business is using all your skills to make
a product or service that people value.

—DARYL BERNSTEIN

From One Kid to Another

Have you always hoped to have enough money to buy what you want? Open a business and you can! You'll earn more money in business than you'll make in allowance over the next fifty years!

In a free country, anyone can open a business—even you. You may believe you can't do anything to make money except deliver newspapers or flip burgers. Change your thinking! Become a part of the free-enterprise system.

When you think of work as a job, you don't look forward to it. Working for yourself and making lots of money is fun! In this book, you won't see the word *job*. Instead, you'll read the words *enterprise* and *venture*, which will remind you of the challenge of starting your own company. Don't get a job. Make a business!

When you earn your own money, it's yours to spend as you wish. Neither this book nor any other should tell you what to do with it. If you decide to save your earnings, great. If you prefer to buy loads of candy, go right ahead. You will have worked hard for your money, so enjoy it. I do!

With the money I've made in business, I've bought a computer, a printer, software, a television, and my own phone. After buying these, I still have enough money to enjoy my favorite hobby: investing in the stock, bond, and options markets.

Some people have said I'm lucky in business, but all it takes is a little common sense. When I see a problem, I charge a fee to solve it. When I see a need, I charge a fee to fill it. Business is really nothing more than one person making life easier for another for a fee. After reading this book, you'll be able to choose your own way of making money by helping others.

Do you think a lemonade stand is the only business you can run? I'll show you fifty-five better ways to make money and have fun while you're at it!

Choose the business that suits you best. Don't expect to make quick bucks. Success takes time. You'll eventually make more money in business than you could make by collecting allowance, delivering newspapers, flipping burgers, or running a lemonade stand!

Daryl

Age 15

Business is a combination of speculation and compensation, and success is simply the desired ratio between the two.

—DARYL BERNSTEIN

Acknowledgments

Writing this book has been one of the most exciting and rewarding experiences of my life. I have been encouraged, educated, and assisted by many people, and I express gratitude to them.

My parents, David and Bianca, are models of determination and inspiration. Besides loving and raising me, they have taught me essential skills for both the business and literary worlds and have prepared me for the world in general. My sister, Sara, has been my closest friend for many years. She helped me develop this book in its early stages. My grandmothers, Gerda and Marian, have been enthusiastic leaders of my fan club. Without my family, my successes would not have been possible.

Richard Cohn and Cynthia Black of Beyond Words were willing to take a risk on a fifteen-year-old kid. Without their belief in me, I would not be an author.

Finally, I want to publicly state my joy about living in a free country where kids can run businesses and even publish books! Thank you, America, for giving me a shot at success.

Cautions

Kids and their parents should carefully read this disclaimer before following any of the suggestions in this book. Neither the author nor the publisher assumes any liability for injuries, whether they be of a physical, psychological, moral, or financial nature, resulting from the use or misuse of this book.

SAFETY

The author has made every reasonable effort to describe safe business ideas for kids. Parents should carefully supervise all activities in which their children engage. Kids are advised to avoid any situation that may be dangerous. Objects that may pose risk include, but are not limited to, ladders, stools, chairs, chemicals, pins, knives, scissors, ovens, bicycles, cars, lawnmowers, snowblowers, hammers, screwdrivers, sewing machines, and shovels. If the business requires travel, meeting with customers in person, or talking with potential clients online, there are risks. Prior to starting a business and as the business grows, kids should consult their parents for advice and supervision.

CHILD LABOR

Both federal and state laws exist concerning child labor. Federal law was updated significantly in the summer of 2010. Neither the author nor the publisher represents that activities suggested for children by the author either adhere or do not adhere to child-labor laws. Parents should research state and federal websites for more information, and should consult their attorneys if they need further guidance to ascertain whether or not their children can legally participate in the business activities described in this book at their ages and in their state of residence.

TAXES

Earned income for children can be taxed by both state and federal governments. Parents should consult a certified public accountant to determine if their children should include tax on their business's products or services and what tax liabilities they might encounter as a result of their children's business activities.

LOCAL ORDINANCES

Some localities prohibit certain types of business activities and require business licenses for others. Check with local authorities to determine if a business described in this book is legal, and is legal for someone your age to participate in, and if a license or permit is needed.

FINANCIAL RISK

All business activities involve some type of financial risk. The author has made every effort to inform kids about limiting expenses. Parents should supervise their children's use of funds in starting and running the small businesses suggested by the author. Kids collecting payment for goods and services are urged to protect themselves against a customer not paying by following standard billing procedures (more on this below). When charging for a service online, it is also important to use whatever is the most recent secure method. Parents and their kids assume all responsibility for monetary losses from use of this book.

FINANCIAL COMPENSATION

This book does not guarantee any type of income. The ideas are perceived opportunities, based on the types of businesses the author ran. However, these have not all been proven and not all ideas will work for everyone. The success of any business depends not only on the opportunity but also on the attitude of the individual and the location where the venture is taking place. For a variety of reasons, many adults may not feel comfortable buying certain products or services from kids. You wouldn't want to sell scuba gear in the desert. You have lots of great ideas, talents, and skills! Spend your energy and time wisely by starting a business where you can see yourself succeeding. Parents and their kids assume all responsibility for any monetary gains from use of this book.

QUIZ:
Are You Ready to Start a Business?

1. **When my alarm clock sounds:**

A. I turn it off and start getting ready for my day, calm, happy, and prepared.

B. I turn it off but dread getting out of bed: I don't know what I need to do that day, and I'm not sure I'll do anything well.

C. I hit the snooze button. And then I hit the snooze button again, and then again...

D. What alarm clock?

2. **When I open my closet door:**

A. I see clean clothes that aren't wrinkled or holey, that are appropriate for my day, and that I like.

B. I'm no fashionista, but I've got some stuff, I can borrow other things from my family and friends, and hey, this is part of why I want to make money—to add to my wardrobe.

C. At least I know where the washing machine and dryer are and how to use an iron.

D. I just grab whatever passes the smell test from my bedroom floor.

3. **When I can't find my favorite brand of gum at the store:**

A. I find a clerk and ask, "Excuse me, can you please help me find Super Bubble?" and after the clerk does, I say thanks.

B. I find a clerk and ask, "Where's the Super Bubble?" Maybe I remember to say thanks.

C. I find a clerk, whoever's closest—it doesn't matter if the clerk is carrying something helpful or talking with another customer—and say, "I can't find the Super Bubble." I take off without thinking to say thank you.

D. As I'm storming out of the store, I yell, "You're so stupid not carrying Super Bubble anymore. I'm never shopping here again, and neither are my friends!"

4. When I forget to put the milk back in the fridge, and it sits on the counter all day:

A. I acknowledge my mistake, apologize to my parents, and run to the store to replace the milk.

B. I make excuses for why I couldn't put the milk back.

C. I blame my sibling.

D. I yell at my parents that they're cheap and that they overreact—it's just milk.

5. It's almost Friday night!

A. I think about what I'd like to do, ask my parents if I need permission or a ride, and coordinate with my friends.

B. I leave all the planning up to my friends.

C. I'm not sure what to do, so I stay home but am happy with that—it's fun at home, and I save money, and there's always next Friday!

D. I feel helpless and hopeless because I don't know what I want to do, and no idea sounds like the exact right one.

6. When I'm around other kids:

A. I manage to find common ground with most people, and I connect with kids who are able to do the same. If there is a problem, we know how to solve it rationally and move on, and when to ask for an adult's advice.

B. I don't always get along with other kids, but I'm trying.

C. I like people who are like me—I don't have patience for other types of people.

D. No one understands me, and I don't understand them.

7. When I'm around adults:

A. I show them respect, and I feel comfortable speaking up with my needs, opinions, and questions.

B. I don't always remember to listen and to ask for clarification, but I'm trying.

C. I only work well with adults who give me what I want.

D. No one understands me, and I don't understand them.

8. **When I look at my schedule for the day and see that I have eight classes and no lunch, soccer practice, and band practice:**

A. Well, first of all, I know my schedule at least one day early. That way I have time to coordinate transportation and make sure I get a good night's sleep the night before. Maybe I even get ahead in homework and chores. I also pack snacks that don't require refrigeration and that are okay to eat on the go. I remember to stay calm during my busy day—maybe drinking plenty of water and doing some locker-room yoga helps—and I don't snap at my family when I get home. They've probably had busy days, too!

B. I grit my teeth and get through it. It's not the best day ever, but it's not the worst—in fact, I do really well on some things—and I don't fall behind for the rest of the week.

C. I realize what my day is going to be like on the way to school that morning, call my mom to see if on her lunch hour she can bring me the soccer cleats I forgot, get more and more anxious as the day goes on, and end up collapsing into bed that night without doing my homework due the next day.

D. What schedule?

Mostly As
It's surprising you haven't started your own business yet! Go for it. With your organization, you can feel free to let your creative energy change your community—and your wallet!—for the better.

Mostly Bs
You could start your own business right now, but consider starting smaller than your ultimate goal, taking time to develop skills and good work habits before you start, or starting a business with a trusted friend or two.

Mostly Cs
You make things happen when you need to, but you rely a lot on other people to do so. You might not have enough experience juggling different activities, or you might have too many in your schedule already. Join a school activity to learn how to manage a more complicated personal schedule, or talk with your parents about dropping one of the activities you currently have. Or be a support for a friend who's trying to be an entrepreneur!

Mostly Ds
For a lot of kids—and adults!—the fun and responsibilities of regular life is enough. Enjoy what you do now, try to improve your habits, and take this quiz again in the future. Now is not the time for you to start your own business, but take some time to think about what you want—you may be ready tomorrow!

6 Lessons for Kid Entrepreneurs

START NOW

Starting a business involves just the right amount of planning. If you do too little, you might make some mistakes that could be easily avoided. If you prepare too much, you can talk yourself out of good ideas and never actually launch your business.

As you consider whether and how to pursue an idea, think about why people will want to buy your product or service, and reasons they won't want to buy it. There will always be both! Talk to friends and family, collect their opinions and suggestions, and find articles online about other entrepreneurs who have started similar businesses.

Remember that there's no such thing as a bad business idea. You can turn *any* idea into a successful business with some creativity, smart decisions, and hard work. Launch your business *now*, and learn as you go.

DREAM BIG

One of the most exciting things about business is the possibility of leverage. This means taking a small success and magnifying it. You prove that your business idea works in your neighborhood, and then you expand it to a bigger geography.

You could be a babysitter. Or you could be a babysitting broker and manage babysitters for your whole town. You could sell your art to friends and neighbors. Or you could create a website and sell your art all over the world.

Every famous company and popular product began as one person's small idea. Your ideas are just as powerful, so start small and dream big!

TALK IT UP

The best way to get your business off the ground is to talk it up! Reach out to friends, friends' parents, family, neighbors, and teachers, and tell them why you started your business and how it can help them.

You'll find that people love to help kid entrepreneurs promote their businesses, and they'll either buy your product or service or introduce you to other people who might buy it.

DON'T BE AFRAID TO FAIL

The only failure you should worry about is failing to try. Most successful entrepreneurs can point to ventures that didn't work out for one reason or another, and many of them will credit those "failures" for helping them learn how not to make the same mistakes in the future. Sometimes a good idea will take several attempts to get right. Sometimes an idea has to be scrapped, but the process of trying it out will lead to new, more fruitful ideas. You just never know until you try.

Also, while many adults are very supportive of kids' ventures, some people will feel a need to "protect" you by warning about how many businesses fail each year, and so on. Don't listen to them! If you plan it out and can see how you might succeed and know you are able to do the work, then go for it! As long as you give your ideas a shot and are willing to use what you learn to help you grow, you will never fail.

AIM FOR WOW

Whatever business you choose, be amazing at it! Create a product that's so good or a service that's so impressive that people are surprised.

If you make cupcakes for birthday parties, decorate them lavishly so partygoers gossip about how beautiful they are. If you landscape, read up on the kinds of plants that grow best in your climate, and show off your knowledge to your customers.

I've met lots of very successful entrepreneurs in my life. Some were smart, and some were lucky. But the one thing they all had in common was that they were *experts* about their businesses, and their product or service made customers say, "Wow!"

ENJOY THE JOURNEY

When you start and run your own business, you'll develop and use skills you didn't know you would ever have. You'll create advertisements, design products, make phone calls, talk to customers, buy supplies, add up revenue and expenses, handle problems, and develop strategies to grow your business.

Sure, it's fun to make money. But the real thrill of business is the adventure along the way: the decisions, challenges, and little victories. Every new customer is an achievement, and every problem you solve makes you a more experienced entrepreneur.

Enjoy the journey of business. Appreciate how you're learning and growing. Savor the satisfaction of turning your idea into a real business using only your smarts, intuition, and good old-fashioned hard work.

Introduction

CHOOSING A BUSINESS

To choose the best business for you, think about your interests. Do you like baseball, animals, young children, puppets, flowers, food, photography, or something else? Flip through this book and find a business that sounds like fun. You don't have to read the information about every business idea, but look at the titles. Read the ones that really appeal to you. Combine business ideas or change them to make them right for you. Talk to owners of similar businesses, especially if they are of a similar size or in a similar location to yours, or just pay attention to those businesses: What seems to be the good and the bad about the work? How do they advertise? How much do they charge? If you enjoy your business, you have a better chance of pleasing your customers and making money.

TRANSPORTATION

In some of the businesses listed, you need to buy supplies or deliver products. A lot of this can happen from the comfort of your own home, via the internet! If you have to travel and if you have a bicycle (and permission), you'll be able to ride to places near your house. To get to locations farther away, you'll need to ask your parents to drive you or if they'll allow you to take the bus. If your parents don't have time or don't want you riding public transportation by yourself, pick a business that doesn't include travel. If you're old enough to drive, you won't have to bother your parents, except to get the keys!

PARTNERS

When you plan to start a small business, you'll want to share your ideas and excitement with friends. You and your friends may decide to go into business as partners. Be careful! Partnerships often wreck businesses—and friendships! If you really want to go into business with someone, be sure your partner is as reliable and hardworking as you are. Sign a contract that outlines the jobs of each person and the division of profits.

INITIAL INVESTMENT

The initial investment is the money you need to start a business. You won't need much money to start the businesses listed in this book. You will need funds to have flyers printed and to buy supplies. If you have money saved up, use it. If you don't have money to spend on initial expenses, you'll need to obtain it. In business, you need to have money to make money!

To get start-up money, try to borrow from your parents. Promise to pay them back, or arrange to do chores in exchange for money.

If your parents, other family members, and friends say no, pitch the investment opportunity to strangers. There are websites that help start-up companies get investments from people all around the world who are interested, and a lot of help can be found via conversations in social media. Or, sell stock in your business. By selling stock, you make investors part owners of your business. For instance, you can sell 1 percent shares in your company for $1 each. When you earn money, you pay each investor 1 percent of your earnings. For instance, if you earn $100, you pay each investor $1. These figures are only examples; you may wish to raise or lower your stock price. Ask local businesspeople to buy shares in your company.

SUPPLIES

Before you buy supplies, ask yourself what you really need. If you can get by without certain items, don't buy them. Once you've decided what you really need, look around your house. If you still need to buy certain supplies, search online or call the stores in your area to find the cheapest prices. Remember, you don't really start making money until you've earned back the cost of your supplies. The cheaper your start-up expenses, the faster you'll turn a profit!

SCHOOL

You may get a little carried away running your small business and forget about school. Remember that school is important, because you need an education to help you succeed when you're older. Keep this in mind, and keep your mind on school.

You may want to let your teachers, coaches, and maybe even your principal know about your business—but not to excuse bad grades or to get extensions on homework. Part of business is networking, or making connections in your community—and your school is part of your community! People in business like to network because sometimes the most exciting opportunities come up with people they know. At your school, for example, if you run a babysitting business and the school thinks more parents would attend football games if their younger children had on-site child care, maybe you could help provide that. Your business might also help you with a school project. A math teacher could be interested in giving extra credit for all the accounting work you're doing in your business, or you might find a topic for your history paper by writing the story of a local business similar to yours. Or, running your own business might fulfill an internship requirement your school has. And, just like you and your parents should be proud of your initiative and hard work, your school will be too!

BUSINESS NAMES

You have to decide on a name for your business. Your name will contribute to your success. Make up a creative name that fits you and your business and that is easy to remember. Customers who like your name are on the way to liking you.

You should also be able to use your business name in your website's address. Ideally, you'll be able to get a URL (your website's address) that uses only your business's name, but that name might be taken by someone else. In that case, make small changes that are still meaningful to your business. For example, if your lawncare service is named Green Machine and you live in Scottsdale, Arizona, you could see if the website address www.greenmachineinscottsdale.com is available. Or you could add the type of service or product you're selling. For example, www.greenmachinelawncare.com.

PRICING

The prices listed for each small business are only suggestions, with many based on a rough national average. Don't hesitate to adjust them if you feel they should be different, and remember to figure in tax if your state requires it or packaging and shipping or transportation reimbursement if you need to send or deliver a product to your customers. Also consider offering discounts or other deals in certain cases. For example, if you babysit more than one child from one family at one time, you might discount your per-child rate. If the client schedules you for repeat projects, you might offer a bulk rate that would be a discount from your regular fee. If you live in an area where lower or higher prices are more appropriate, change them accordingly.

NEGOTIATION

Some customers will try to bargain with you. You have two options. You can refuse to deal and potentially lose the customer, or you can lower your price. Don't hesitate to negotiate, because in business almost all deals are made through bargaining. In the first stage of negotiation, don't lower your price too much. For instance, if you charge $7.50 per hour for your work and a potential customer offers to pay you $5 per hour, make a counteroffer of $6.75 per hour. The customer may then raise the bid to $6 per hour. When the bargaining is finished, perhaps you will have settled on a fee of $6.25 per hour. It's better to make a dollar less per hour than nothing at all if you can still cover your expenses and are happy with what is left over.

AGREEMENTS

Just as you should prepare and sign a contract with any business partners or investors, for certain services you should have a formal agreement with your customers. It can be very simple but should describe the service or product, any deadlines, cost, and payment expectations. (Try looking online for some contract examples.) You and the client should sign and date two copies of your agreement and each of you should keep a copy.

ADVERTISING

Advertising is simply the process of letting people know about your business. Big companies spend large amounts of money for advertisements on television and radio. There are cheaper ways to spread the word about your enterprise. The main methods suggested in this book are the internet, paper advertisements like flyers, brochures, or business cards, and in-person sales.

When you start the business, count on the extra hours you'll need to spend advertising. Also, not all businesses need the same level of advertising. You should do as much or as little as you want or that fits your type of product or service—and you can always adjust later. Create a unique, clear design that fits your business and that you can use online and on paper.

With your parents' permission, set up a website and get accounts on social media sites. You can make a website simply and for free by using one of the blogging hosts that also offer ready-made website templates.

For most businesses, flyers, brochures, or business cards can help. If you have a computer, printer, and design software, you can create these on your computer. If you're a good artist, you can draw, but be neat and make the words readable. If you don't have a computer or artistic talent, you can ask a friend or your school's graphic design club or marketing class, or you can go to your local print shop and pay to have the materials designed.

Once your brochures or cards are designed, make photocopies or have them printed. If you're planning to make fewer than a hundred copies, photocopies will be cheapest. If your parents have access to a copy machine at work, ask if they could make copies. Otherwise, have the photocopies made at a local print shop. If you plan to have more than a few hundred copies made, printing will be the most convenient. Research online different paper types, color, and pricing options. Find several print shops in town and call or visit them online to find the cheapest prices. When you're asking about pricing, learn about the same type of printing each time in order to make accurate comparisons. Be sure your flyer is striking, because it will create a first impression. Ask the print shop if you can preview the flyer before the full order is printed, so you can catch any mistakes or make any adjustments.

To publicize your business properly, use repeat advertising. People will most likely remember the name of your business if they see it repeatedly. Avoid bothering people by making a lot of your marketing like a conversation, rather than a sales pitch, and by sharing the same message in different ways. Always include your business name and a way to contact you, but sometimes offer tips, news items, or funny stories related to your work. Ask for other people's stories or questions, which will lead to conversation, and promote other businesses, which will lead to them promoting your work! Update your website and social media accounts regularly, and ask other people if you can write a guest post for their site.

Post photos or drawings of your product or service and videos and podcasts of you working, but be aware of copyright—yours and other people's. If you hold the copyright to something, you own it, which means you, and only you, decide how it's used.

Things that have copyright include writing, photos, artwork, music, television, and movies. Usually, the creator of the work holds the copyright. You may have heard people talking about the copyright of online music and movies. If you download a song without the owner's permission (often meaning, without paying for the song), you may be in violation of the copyright, and that is illegal. A lot of times you will see the copyright symbol, ©, by something that is owned, but not always. So, you own the copyright to everything you write on your website. When in doubt, ask permission to talk about someone else or their work.

Also ask customers who you know are pleased with your work whether they would be willing to write an online review or social media message, or to give you a quote you could use in your advertising materials.

Although online and print advertising can bring you business, nothing is more impressive to potential customers than in-person advertising. When you attend a business event or visit homes and businesses, you have the opportunity to show customers your winning personality. You have the chance to present your business, observe the potential client's reaction, and convince the listener of the value of your product. Before you meet with people, plan a sales pitch and practice it thoroughly.

ORGANIZATION

To succeed in business, you must be very organized. If you run an enterprise that requires scheduled appointments, write them on a calendar and check it every day. Use client information sheets to help you remember your customers' specific needs. If you ever forget a commitment, you risk losing not only one client but all the future customers that person might have referred to you.

If you're using a computer or cell phone, you can ask your customers to order or share their information with you electronically, so your files update automatically or to make your transfer of the information easier. You can also schedule reminders for yourself.

Set up online email accounts that are separate from your personal accounts. In addition to helping with organization, it also makes your business appear more established to people.

Remember to back everything up regularly! It's a good idea to make a copy of your work at the end of each day and then another copy at the end of each week or month. You can back up to separate computer hard drives or internet servers; if you're pressed for time and you use a web-based email, you can even email yourself your documents for temporary safekeeping.

COURTESY

When communicating with customers, always be professional, even when you're being informal. Courtesy impresses customers. Address a client using "Sir" or "Ma'am," or the last name with "Mr." or "Ms." Don't call your customers by their first names, unless they have specifically asked you to do so. By treating people with respect, you'll get more business.

You've probably heard the expression, "The customer is always right." Follow this rule and you'll never offend clients. You may become impatient if customers criticize your work or ask you to redo a task but try not to express frustration. Mistakes happen and people miscommunicate all the time. If someone is unhappy with you, treat it as a learning experience. Work with your clients to determine how to best correct the mistake or compromise so both of you are happy. Just as you may have had to negotiate price, you may have to negotiate so the client is pleased and so that you don't get pushed into doing extra work or work not in the original contract. You might need to redo the work for free or you might be able to offer a discount on future work. Ask your parents, teachers, or other trusted adults for help, if you want to, before addressing a customer's concern. Also be sure to use unhappy customers' feedback to help you protect against future problems. If they misunderstood something you said and expect you to do something you didn't plan to, it might be easier to do it this time, but remember to be more careful to set clear expectations next time and with your next customer.

Another saying is, "One happy customer leads to another." When your customers are pleased, they refer you to their friends. The only good customer is a happy one. If your customers are pleased with you, they will use you again, and your business will be successful. Some entrepreneurs offer a discount to customers for referring others to them.

To impress your clients, give small gifts to remind them of your service. Send greeting cards before the holidays. If you run a neighborhood business, give each customer a small pumpkin at Halloween. Think of other ways to keep your customers satisfied. Remember, happy customers enjoy spending money and telling their friends to spend money!

CUSTOMERS

Doing business with strangers is usually easier than doing business with family and friends. Family and friends sometimes expect you to perform services for free. Strangers, on the other hand, assume they will pay for your work. If conflicts arise in deals with friends, you might ruin a relationship. If they occur with strangers, you might lose a customer but not a friend. Therefore, try to avoid dealing with people close to you. If you do work with people you know, treat them like a client you don't know when you're doing business with them.

BILLING

Billing is sending notices, or invoices, requesting payment for services performed or products sold. You can bill and accept payment in person, by mail, or online, but it's always a good idea to keep a written record. There are easy ways for the smallest of businesses to receive payment online, which is often the most efficient way. Make sure you and your parents have researched such services so that both you and your customers will feel safe and comfortable using it, test that you download or install it correctly, and just because it won't produce paper doesn't mean you should ignore it—check your account regularly and don't forget to back it up often!

In your initial contract with a customer, explain when you expect payment. Payment upon receipt of an invoice is common. You may also want to ask for a nonrefundable deposit of 10 percent before you start the project. That way, your client has made a financial commitment, and you've earned something right away or have some money to put toward supplies needed for the project.

Often, customers won't send payment quickly. Therefore, you need to send extra notices. Keep careful track of when you send out bills. If you haven't received payment after ten days, send the first notice. In it, remind the customers that they owe you money. If you still haven't received payment after another ten days, send another notice. This time, sound a bit more serious but maintain a courteous tone. Continue sending notices until you receive payment—making each a little more demanding than the previous one. Calling the customers may help to expedite the process. If you continue to not hear from a client, or if a client refuses to pay, talk with an adult about taking your problem to a collections agency or lawyer. You may also have to accept not getting paid for this job, in which case you have learned a lot, including not to work with that customer again.

Usually, though, everything works out fine. Remember to open a bank account that you can deposit cash, checks, or money from credit cards into—you're about to start earning money!

SUCCESS

Nothing feels as good as putting your mind to something and succeeding. You'll face obstacles when going into business. Overcoming them is the goal. Business is a challenge, so any amount of money you earn, whether large or small, represents an achievement. You will always gain business and life experience, and that will help you in school now, applying to college or other programs later, and working as an adult. You may even start more businesses later. Enterprise can disappoint, dishearten, and discourage, but experience and success makes it all worthwhile!

QUIZ:
Which Business Is Right for You?

The following questions ask the same thing in different ways—to help you figure out what business you may enjoy and be good at. All of the suggested businesses are described in more detail later in the book.

1. Which do you think you have the most of?

* If you have a lot of **determination**, you might try being a Flyer Distributor, Garbage Can Mover, Newspaper Mover, Price Shopper, or Seedling Grower.

* A Cage or Litter Box Cleaner, Dog Walker, or Elderly Helper is a good task for kids who are full of **kindness**.

* If you are **charismatic**, you might want to be a Birthday Party Planner, Disc Jockey, Face Painter, or Wake-Up Caller.

* **Imagination** is an important trait for Balloon-Bouquet Makers, Button Makers, and Store Window Painters.

* With a **fun** personality, you might be a great Gift Wrapper, Party Helper, or Photographer.

* Use your **smarts** as a Homework Helper, Newspaper Publisher, Online Advisor, or Website Designer.

* **Strength** is helpful if you want to be a Car Washer, Dry Cleaning Deliverer, Grocery Deliverer, Landscaper, Leaf Raker, Snow Shoveler.

2. If you could be a beverage, what kind would you be?

Water

* Maybe you care about the **environment**—you could be a Recycler, Landscaper, or Leaf Raker.

* Or maybe you are an **athlete**—work your muscles as a Car Washer, Coupon Booklet Distributor, Curb Address Painter, Dog Walker, Flyer Distributor, New-Product Assembler, or Window Washer.

Anything with caffeine!

* You might **like staying up late**—be a Babysitting Broker, Disc Jockey, Grocery Deliverer, Homework Helper, House Checker, Online Advisor, Online Seller, Party Helper, or Website Designer.

Anything without caffeine!

* You **shine when you rise** every morning—you could be a Cake Baker, Elderly Helper, Garbage Mover, Leaf Raker, Muffin and Juice Deliverer, Newspaper Mover, or Wake-Up Caller.

Juice

* You like the **sweeter things** in life—try being a Cake Baker, Fresh-Flower Deliverer, Gift-Basket Maker, Jewelry Maker, Muffin and Juice Deliverer, Mural Painter, Photograph Organizer, Puppet Maker, Rock Painter, or Snack Vendor.

Hot chocolate

* Maybe you like to try things that are a **little different**—you could be a Collectibles Show Organizer, Document Preparer, New-Product Assembler, Online Seller, Puppet Maker, Rock Painter, Shirt Designer, Silver Polisher, Street Flower Vendor, or Tech Teacher.

Milk

* Maybe you are good at **comforting**—be a Dog Walker, Elderly Helper, Fresh-Flower Deliverer, Gift-Basket Maker, Gift Wrapper, Grocery Deliverer, Homework Helper, Sheet and Towel Washer, or Wake-Up Caller.

3. There are people in your community who have nothing. If you could give one thing to them, what would it be?

* If you think **shelter** is most important, consider being a House Checker, Leaf Raker, Sheet and Towel Washer, or Window Washer.

* An interest in **food** might mean you could be a successful Birthday Party Planner, Cake Baker, Gift-Basket Maker, or Muffin and Juice Deliverer.

* If you agree that every living thing does better if they can relax and enjoy a little **entertainment**, be a Balloon-Bouquet Maker, Disc Jockey, Dog Walker, Elderly Helper, or Rock Painter.

* **Education** might be your key—be a Coupon Booklet Distributor, Document Preparer, Flyer Distributor, Homework Helper, New-Product Assembler, Newsletter

Publisher, Online Advisor, Photograph Organizer, Price Shopper, Seedling Grower, Phone Information-Line Organizer, Tech Teacher, or Website Designer.

* **Medical care** can span a wide spectrum of important needs—make your mark by being a Cage or Litter Box Cleaner, Elderly Helper, Grocery Deliverer, New-Product Assembler, Newsletter Publisher, Price Shopper, Seedling Grower, or Sheet and Towel Washer.

* If you have an interest in **transportation**, start a business as a Car Washer, Coupon Booklet Distributor, Curb Address Painter, Dog Walker, Dry Cleaning Deliverer, Flyer Distributor, Fresh-Flower Deliverer, or Grocery Deliverer.

4. What is your favorite subject in school? You may be surprised at what businesses that subject shows up in.

* Math: Collectibles Show Organizer, Cake Baker, Landscaper

* Science: Recycler, Rock Painter, Silver Polisher, Seedling Grower, Snow Shoveler

* Reading: Document Preparer, Elderly Helper

* Art: Photograph Organizer, Sign Maker, Store Window Painter

* Music: Disc Jockey, Elderly Helper, Party Helper

* Gym: Snow Shoveler, Window Washer

* Lunch: Cake Baker, Grocery Deliverer, Muffin and Juice Deliverer, Snack Vendor

* Recess: Garbage Mover, Landscaper, Leaf Raker, Newspaper Mover, Recycler

* Social studies/History: Document Preparer, Newsletter Publisher, Phone Information-Line Organizer, Photographer, Price Shopper

* The club or sport you are in after school: House Checker, Puppet Maker, Silver Polisher

* The TV or video games you play before and after school: Elderly Helper, Tech Teacher

1

Babysitting Broker

*While your sitters take care of kids,
you'll take care of business!*

You arrange babysitting services for parents in your neighborhood. You act as a babysitting broker by hiring other kids to babysit.

SUPPLIES

You will need a phone or computer and advertising.

TIME NEEDED

To start up, you need to find a few responsible babysitters who have good references, and you need to find some parents looking for reliable babysitting services. When you are ready to start, allow time to communicate with parents seeking babysitters, contact other kids to babysit, check on babysitters while they are working, and follow up with parents to make sure they are satisfied. You may have to babysit when one of your babysitters gets sick or doesn't show up at the scheduled time. Make yourself available on babysitting nights for such occurrences.

WHAT TO CHARGE

Bill the parents $12 per hour. Pay the babysitter $10 per hour. You make $2 per hour. That may not sound like a lot, but if the babysitter works for three hours, you make $6. If you have five babysitters working one evening, you make $30 and don't even leave your house!

HOW TO ADVERTISE

As soon as you have parents who are using your service, ask them for a quote about your business to include in your advertising. Ask neighborhood coffee shops, grocery stores, and libraries if you can post flyers or business cards on their community bulletin boards. Advertise in your school's, club's, team's, and community or religious center's newsletters. Talk about your business on your website and by commenting in other people's online discussions. Explain that a reliable, friendly babysitter will be available on the night parents request. Emphasize that parents should contact you at least three days before the requested time to arrange for a sitter, and mention that you take calls and answer emails only in the evening, because you attend school. Don't forget to tell your friends' parents in person when you go over to their house.

HINTS

* You might consider offering higher "last-minute" prices for people who have sudden need for a babysitter and can't give advance notice.
* Tell older kids in your area that you would like to find them babysitting work. If they want to participate, have them write their name, address, phone number, and email address on a list. Be sure to pick responsible kids. Find kids who will show up for work and be kind and attentive to young children. Create and sign a detailed agreement with your sitters.
* Also create and sign a detailed agreement with your parent clients, especially noting what they need to pay if they cancel at the last minute. When parents call you, write down the date and time the sitter is needed, the address of the house, and the ages of the children. Call a babysitter on your list and convey the necessary information. Notify the parents to tell them the name of, and something about, the babysitter you have scheduled.
* On the day of the appointment, call the babysitter to be sure that person doesn't forget! Remind babysitters to note the number of hours they babysit but not to collect any money. You will bill parents and pay the babysitter.
* To be successful in this business, you must please parents. Follow up babysitting sessions with a phone call or email. This business requires paperwork and phone calls, but you can make money without leaving your home.

INSPIRATION FROM KID ENTREPRENEURS JUST LIKE YOU!

NAME: Farrhad Acidwalla

TITLE: entrepreneur, CEO

AGE: 17

WHERE: India

WHAT: Farrhad is all things PR, founding and running Rockstah Media, which helps corporations strengthen their online and offline presence.

HOW: From $10 borrowed from his parents four years ago to now, Farrhad has become an internet mogul, buying, developing, and then selling for a profit several websites. With these as stepping stones to ever bigger success, Farrhad founded Rockstah. And he still finds time to study, as a student at H. R. College of Commerce & Economics.

FUN FACT: Rockstah Media's one goal, according to its website: "Creating Awesomeness." Awesome.

RESOURCE: www.rockstahmedia.com

2

Balloon-Bouquet Maker

Up, up, and away!

You make balloon bouquets that are similar to flower bouquets in arrangement and decoration. Customers will need your balloons for parties, conferences, displays, and similar events. You inflate balloons, and customers pick them up from your house or you deliver them.

SUPPLIES

You will need a phone or computer, a helium tank, balloons and ribbons, and advertising. You can purchase a new or used small helium tank, balloons, ribbons, and other decorations online or at a warehouse-style store or a party supply company. If your business gets big, look into buying the balloons from wholesalers.

TIME NEEDED

Inflating the balloons takes little time—about one minute per balloon. Deliver the balloons within twenty-four hours of inflating them, before they lose air.

WHAT TO CHARGE

Charge $1 per balloon for simple arrangements, and $2 per balloon for fancier styles. If customers want the balloons filled with air instead of helium, charge 25 cents less.

HOW TO ADVERTISE

Attach your flyers or business cards to balloons and distribute them at fairs, school events, sporting events, and other public occasions. Children will want your free balloons. As you give them to kids, describe your balloon-bouquet service to parents.

With the owners' permission, leave stacks of your flyers on the counters of local party supply and costume rental stores. Party hosts will pick up the flyers and call you. Do the same at hotels and conference centers in your area. When businesspeople organize conferences and meetings, they often need balloons to make the setting more lively.

Increase your advertising around official holidays such as New Year's Eve and general times of celebration such as June, when students graduate. People have parties at holidays and need balloons.

HINTS

* Balloons are cheap. The best way to spread the word about your business is to give away free balloons at events in different parts of town. Always attach something with your business name and contact information to the balloons. People will love the balloons, and you get to advertise.
* Customers might call with a request for a theme balloon bouquet. For instance, they might plan a party with a flamingo theme. In this case, you would offer pink and white balloons. The more creative you are in arranging the bouquets, the more business you will have.

3

Birthday Party Planner

Help parents put on the best birthday party ever!

If you enjoy young children, this business will be fun. You plan birthday parties from invitations and setup to food, entertainment, and gift bags.

SUPPLIES

You will need a phone or computer, advertising, a clown or magician's outfit, and magic tricks. You can make outfits from old clothes and buy a complete magic kit online or in a store that sells toys. You may even be able to find a used kit online—just make sure the magic hasn't already been used up!

TIME NEEDED

Each party lasts two to four hours. People hold most parties on weekends.

WHAT TO CHARGE

Charge $10 per child. The birthday child is free. For example, if the birthday child is inviting ten other children, the parents of the birthday child will pay you $100. Remind parents that the fee includes food, prizes, and gift bags.

HOW TO ADVERTISE

Advertise your services by asking elementary school teachers to hand out your flyers to their classes. The students will take the flyers home and show them to parents. Elementary schools often have student directories or newsletters in which you can advertise. Contact schools in the summer to find out the publication date of the directory and cost of an advertisement. Mention in your flyers and advertisements that parents should call you at least three weeks before their child's birthday so you have time to plan the party.

HINTS

* Meet with parents well in advance of the child's birthday. Before your meeting, make a list of themes, games, and foods from which parents can choose. Popular themes are baseball, car racing, video games, horses, dolls, and flowers. Discuss all aspects of the party and take careful notes. Select the date, time, and length of the party. Establish the theme according to the child's interests. Decide which foods will be served, what types of games will be fun, and whether you will perform a magic show. Because this business requires you to spend money before each time you make money, collect half the money at the meeting and the other half after the party. Tell parents you need the money to pay for supplies.

* Between the meeting and the party, spend time looking for the cheapest food, paper plates, utensils, and prizes. The less you spend on supplies, the more money you make! Remember to pay some attention to quality (if you're having messy foods, you don't want them to soak through the paper) and to the environment (sometimes you will have to balance environmentally friendly materials and cost, but if you do some research into your options, you may not have to compromise too much). As you purchase materials for the party, check them off in your notes so you don't forget anything.

* On the day of the party, arrive at least half an hour early to set the table and decorate the room. After the party, clean up and give parents five of your flyers for their friends. Collect the rest of your money!

4

Button Maker

The more buttons people pin,
the more money you'll win!

You produce buttons for local businesses that use them for promotions and other functions. Business owners give you the designs and tell you the quantity of buttons needed. You can also make buttons other kids will want to wear as fashion. You have the designs printed on paper and use a special tool to assemble each button.

SUPPLIES

You will need a phone or computer, advertising, and a button-making device that will cost as little as $25 to $30. If you're making your own designs, you can use clippings from old magazines.

TIME NEEDED

For buttons that another business will use as advertising, you may want to have their logo or button design professionally printed. Set aside thirty minutes to talk with the print shop about having the design printed. You will have to return at a later date to pick up the printed copies. Plan on a minute per button for assembly.

WHAT TO CHARGE

Charge 50 cents more per button than your cost. For instance, if the supplies for each button cost you 25 cents, charge your customer 75 cents. Set a minimum order of fifty buttons. If you make a profit of 50 cents per button, you will earn a minimum of $25!

HOW TO ADVERTISE

Visit local business owners and present them with sample buttons that display your name, service, and phone number. Wear a variety of colorful buttons on your clothes when you go out to advertise. As an introductory offer, say you'll make five free buttons for every fifty ordered.

Schools have clubs that need to advertise. Club participants recruit members and publicize events by wearing buttons. Offer your service to clubs at schools by attending afterschool meetings.

HINTS

* Potential customers will want to see samples of your work. Make extra buttons to create a portfolio.
* Once you have several satisfied clients, use them as referrals. You can persuade potential customers by having them contact references who will praise the quality of your work.
* Consider setting up a booth at a fair and making picture buttons. You do everything from taking the photos of the fairgoers to making the buttons while the customers wait or shop at the other booths. You may need to hire an assistant so you can keep up with fast and simultaneous selling and making. Or let customers submit photos online for a virtual fair! Charge $5 for the first button and $3 for duplicates.
* Some organizations may consider using buttons as identification badges to display photos of their employees. Security companies may want identification buttons for their security guards, and theaters and stadiums can use them for their ushers.
* Experiment with materials, too—for example, you can make some great buttons by gluing safety pins to the backs of bottle caps.

5

Cage or Litter Box Cleaner

Soon, you'll need a cage to
hold all your money!

Many people have birds, hamsters, gerbils, rabbits, cats, and other animals as pets, but they don't like to clean cages or litter boxes. You offer to clean them, empty trays, and do other chores related to pet care.

SUPPLIES

You will need a phone or computer, advertising, plastic bags, and old rags, a bucket for water, and animal-safe soap. Watch for sales online or at hardware stores, so you can buy supplies cheaply. Look for old rags and a bucket around your house.

TIME NEEDED

Cleaning and emptying a cage or litter box takes about forty-five minutes. Large cages require longer. Allow time to go door-to-door to present your service to potential clients.

WHAT TO CHARGE

$7.25 per cleaning. Remind the customer that you supply the cleaning materials.

HOW TO ADVERTISE

Knock on doors in your neighborhood and introduce yourself. Explain your service and ask if the homeowner has animal cages or litter boxes. If the answer is yes, describe in more detail what you do. If someone is unsure about hiring you, offer to clean a cage or box once for free. When the homeowner sees the quality of your work, you will have a permanent customer. If the answer is no, say, "Thank you anyway. Do you have friends or neighbors with animal cages or litter boxes?" People without cages can be helpful, because they may give you referrals.

Ask the owner of your local pet store if you can leave business cards on the front desk. You can request that the owner give each person who purchases a cage or litter box one of your business cards. If you have difficulty getting a pet store merchant to cooperate, point out that potential animal owners might be more likely to make purchases if they know they won't have to clean their animals' cages.

Never forget your online advertising as well!

HINTS

* On the first visit, ask each customer to explain how the cage or box is to be cleaned. If you feel an animal is dangerous, ask its owner to remove it from the area before you begin to clean. When you finish, leave one of your business cards in the back corner of the cage or sticking out from under the box. Collect your money and ask if you can come at the same time every week to clean the cage.

* Try a personal touch to please owners. Buy a small bell no larger than a half-inch and attach it to a ribbon. Give the gift to an owner of a bird to hang in the cage. The sound of the bell will make the bird sing and will remind the owner of your excellent service. For owners of rabbits, bring a carrot. A happy animal can mean repeat business!

* Remember to take care when choosing cleansers, because certain kinds are harmful to animals. Check with your local pet store to find out which ones are best.

INSPIRATION FROM KID ENTREPRENEURS JUST LIKE YOU!

NAME: Stanley Tang

TITLE: writer, web entrepreneur

AGE: 18

WHERE: California, USA; Hong Kong

WHAT: The better question is, what hasn't Stanley worked on? Currently, he's focusing on his company BuzzBlaze, a social news aggregation website, and his book *eMillions: Behind-The-Scenes Stories of 14 Successful Internet Millionaires*, which was originally published in 2008, when he was just fifteen years old.

HOW: Stanley caught the entrepreneurial bug early. At age eleven, he noticed that his fellow students both didn't like most of the snack options on sale at school and didn't have enough time to visit the convenience store on breaks during the day. So he bought snacks after school and then sold them to his classmates for a profit the next day.

FUN FACT: You can download a free e-copy of Stanley's book here: http://emillionsbook.com/stdownload.html. What a great marketing idea, Stanley!

RESOURCE: www.stanleytang.com

18

6

Cake Baker

Put on your chef's hat and bake up a storm!

Party hosts order cakes from you. Weddings, birthdays, and anniversaries are occasions for which people need cakes. If you are an excellent baker, this business is for you!

SUPPLIES

You will need a phone or computer, advertising, an oven, a mixer or food processor, and other cooking supplies. You should have cake boxes, too, which can be purchased from a baking-supply company.

TIME NEEDED

Baking and decorating a cake takes at least two and a half hours. This includes the time the cake is in the oven. Set aside extra time to go to the market and buy your supplies. If your customers want delivery service, you will need to spend time getting to and from their location.

WHAT TO CHARGE

Depending on the size of the cake, charge between $15 and $30. For large cakes, consider charging more.

HOW TO ADVERTISE

Advertise in person, with flyers, and online, focusing on party-supply stores, hotels and conference centers, schools and day cares. People buying other supplies for a party will call you to order a cake, businesspeople often need treats for their meetings, and parents and teachers buy cakes for parties, fund-raisers, and other school-related events.

HINTS

* When customers contact you, ask for their name, address, and phone number and email address. Ask them what flavor the cake should be, if they have any food allergies or dietary needs, and how it is to be decorated. Include a business card with your

finished cake or, if your business gets big, have stickers printed with your name and contact information on them and put them on the cake boxes.

* You have to be an experienced baker to run this business. If you're not, check out cookbooks from your library or watch how-to videos online. Sometimes even television food shows and competitions can offer some advice! Ask someone you know who is good at baking to help you learn.

* Make your cakes unique. Try using different letter styles and colors. Consider unusual slogans. If a cake has a theme, look for decorations to go with it. Offer unusually flavored cakes, such as raspberry, peach, dulce de leche, or monster (lots of different ingredients in one cake). If the honored guest at the event is a kid, remember that most kids love frosting, so be generous with it!

* Many people are watching their health. Find books or websites that offer low-calorie, low-fat, low-sugar, vegan, and other specialized recipes. Since some people have serious health conditions caused by gluten, you should probably not offer gluten-free options. These require a separate kitchen where all wheat flour has been cleaned from every surface. Many kids have nut allergies, and those, too, are serious. It's probably best to avoid using nuts because it's so easy to accidentally transfer nut dust from one cake to another.

* If your cakes are excellent, you may be able to sell them to restaurants. Civic organizations may be interested in buying cakes, too. This type of selling can be big business.

INSPIRATION FROM KID ENTREPRENEURS JUST LIKE YOU!

NAME: Ben Yu

TITLE: adventurer, entrepreneur

AGE: 19

WHERE: California, USA

WHAT: Ben is trying to revolutionize online price comparison by developing a product search engine that reliably takes into account coupons and other limited-time offers.

HOW: Ben took a break from his undergraduate studies at Harvard University because he realized he didn't know what he wanted to study for four years, and the general core curriculum required of freshmen wasn't helping him make that decision. His first plan was to travel the world, and he did a little of that, including climbing Mt. Kilimanjaro, but then he applied for and received a 20 Under 20 Fellowship, and is now settled in San Francisco to work on his project.

FUN FACT: "My favorite color was green, but I decided to alter my allegiance to **white** sometime during sophomore year of high school, so that I could claim ultimate favoritism of all colors."

RESOURCE: http://benyu.org; http://hpronline.org/interviews/ben-yu-harvard-dropout-and-thiel-fellow; http://thielfoundation.org/index.php?option=com_content&id=15

Car Washer

Wishy-washy
buckets of fun!

You make dirty cars clean. You not only wash the car but offer extra services such as waxing, interior cleaning, and tire polishing.

SUPPLIES

You will need a pushcart, bucket, and liquid soap. You can make rags from clean old T-shirts, cloth baby diapers, and towels. If you offer waxing, you will need wax, extra rags, and a chamois cloth. For interior cleaning, you may want dashboard spray, air freshener, a hand vacuum, and similar specialty items.

TIME NEEDED

Spend an hour on each car, or more time if you're doing extra services. This business works well on weekends, because people are generally too busy during the week to bother with having their car washed.

WHAT TO CHARGE

$20 to $30 per car, and more for extra services. Remind your customers that you supply the cleaning materials.

HOW TO ADVERTISE

You can distribute flyers, but door-to-door advertising works better in this business. Ring a doorbell, and when someone answers, introduce yourself. Say you would like to wash the person's car. Emphasize that you have all the supplies except water. When you finish washing the car, give the customer five of your flyers and mention that you look forward to returning soon. The customer will save one of your flyers and give the others to friends who might want to hire you.

While you wash cars, put a sign near the street so drivers of cars passing by will read about your business. Your sign might say: "Car washing and detailing. Quick service. Cheap prices. Call Otto Bright at 123-4567 or email Otto@email.com."

HINTS

* Be really careful to use cloths that are recommended for exteriors. Scrubbing a car the wrong way with the wrong cloth can ruin a paint job, which is extremely expensive to fix. You can also ask your customers what they prefer to use but either way be sure to ask at your local automotive store and go for quality.
* Offer to do it once a week or to wash a customer's second car at a discounted rate. Remember, customers love special deals!
* There are several easy steps in washing a car thoroughly. Squirt liquid soap in a bucket. Rinse the car quickly, using the customer's hose, and fill the bucket with water. The water should be sudsy. Dip your sponge or cleaning cloth in it and gently wash the car in a circular motion. Pay attention to cracks and crevices that need cleaning. Rinse the soap off the car using the hose. Use two or three clean rags to dry the car completely. Presto, you're done!

* When cleaning the interior of a car, be careful not to spill solutions on the fabric. Take care not to damage your customers' personal belongings, such as sunglasses or briefcases. If you spot expensive gadgets in the car, ask the customers to remove them before you begin cleaning.

* When you finish, leave one of your flyers on the dashboard with a small chocolate mint (unless it's summer, in which case use something that doesn't melt!). A gesture like this can bring you repeat business and more money.

* Research the products you should buy and the steps you should take to make your car washing more environmentally friendly.

8

Collectibles Show Organizer

You won't strike out with this business!

You organize shows for collectors in school gymnasiums or cafeterias. Kids rent tables to sell things they collect to other collectors. They pay you for space at your show. Think of all the types of collector's items: comic books, video games, records and CDs, model cars and trains, baseball cards, stuffed toys and dolls, and many more. You could host one show for multiple collections, but you'll probably find more success if you focus your show on one type.

SUPPLIES

You will need a phone or computer and advertising. To run the show, you will have to locate tables for kids to rent. You can rent tables cheaply from a party-supply company if the schools don't supply them.

TIME NEEDED

You need to start planning a show at least six months in advance. The show can be one day long, on a Saturday, or it can last two days, over a weekend. Most shows are from nine in the morning to six in the evening.

WHAT TO CHARGE

Organizing a show can be a little tricky, but it won't be a problem if you write everything down. You have to find out the cost of renting school space. You may want to offer a portion of your profits to the school as a donation in exchange for a cheaper rate. Make calls to find the cheapest price in town. Pick the date of the show and make a reservation for the room. Arrange to pay for the room after you receive payment from kids. To determine the price to charge kids to rent tables, double the cost of the room and divide by the number of tables that fit into the room. For example, you reserve a room that holds twenty tables. The cost of the room is $200 for the day. You double the cost of the room and get $400. You divide $400 by twenty to get $20. You rent the tables to kids for $20 each. For organizing this show, you'd earn $200!

HOW TO ADVERTISE

Distribute flyers to every kid you know who has a collection of whatever type of item your show will sell. Here's an example of a flyer: "Kids, have you always wanted to have your own table at a comic book show? For only $20, you can! There will be a show by and for kids at Stephens Middle School cafeteria on May 5 from 9 a.m. to 6 p.m. Call 123-4567 or email firstname@businessname.com to reserve a table."

To advertise your show to the public, leave flyers in stores and post online. Remind the owners of businesses that sell collector's memorabilia that shows like yours bring them business!

HINTS

* If you are organizing the show, don't pay the school before you receive payment from kids. If you follow the pricing schedule described above, you will have to rent half the tables to break even. To make money, you will need to rent more than half the tables.
* If you find that the schools in your area are too expensive or are unwilling to rent space, try local hotels and convention centers. Their fees may be high, so raise your prices accordingly.

INSPIRATION FROM KID ENTREPRENEURS JUST LIKE YOU!

NAME: Carl Ocab

TITLE: moneymaker

AGE: 16

WHERE: Philippines

WHAT: Nicknamed Kidblogger, Carl blogs about making money online—and in the process has caught the eye of some serious adult internet marketing experts.

HOW: What started one of those lazy addictions we all have—for Carl, it was playing online games all day—led to Carl doing some serious thinking. Spending all his time, and money, on chatting and gaming as a ten-year-old wasn't the best thing for him, but it did show that he was passionate about technology and networking. His dad clued him in to the idea of blogging for money.

FUN FACT: A fun quote from Carl: "I don't treat internet marketing or blogging as school . . . It's a playground. Where you can learn from other kids' mistakes by looking at what they're playing with. You learn while you enjoy" (http://deanhunt.com/carl-ocab-too-cool-for-school-night/).

RESOURCE: www.carlocab.com

9

Coupon Booklet Distributor

*50 percent off means
more in your pockets!*

You call or visit local business owners and ask them to buy a coupon advertisement in your booklet. When you've collected enough advertisers, you have the booklets printed and distribute them to the houses in your neighborhood.

SUPPLIES

You will need a phone or computer and depending on how many booklets you print at one time, a place to store them before you deliver them.

TIME NEEDED

You will need to spend about two months selling advertising space in your booklet. To do this, you will have to make many phone calls and sales visits. You email businesses, but voice is still important in making such sales. Distributing the booklets to houses in your neighborhood will take at least a day.

WHAT TO CHARGE

Charge each advertiser $30 to have a coupon in your booklet. If you produce a twenty-page booklet, you can collect $600! Remember, you won't keep all of that, because you have to pay for the printing of the coupons.

HOW TO ADVERTISE

You can get business owners to advertise in your coupon booklet by calling or visiting them and describing your service. Be sure to mention the number of houses to which the booklet will be distributed. You have to convince advertisers that coupons will bring them many customers. Make an effective sales pitch. Emphasize that you will personally deliver the booklets to houses. Promise to show the advertiser the coupon booklet before you have it printed.

Guarantee that the booklet will be distributed on a certain day. Assure business owners that you will verify that the booklets reach the public.

HINTS

* Collect half the money when you first get a new customer. This money will go toward your printing costs. Collect the other half after you distribute the booklets.
* If you can't design the coupons, ask business owners to supply the design. You may have to charge less if you don't design the coupons.
* Be sure to put your name and phone number on each coupon, so potential customers who see the booklet can call you and buy advertising space in the next edition. But don't let your business overshadow your clients'!
* Have the print shop print eight coupons per page. Cut and staple the pages to make booklets.
* If the cost isn't too high, try to have the coupons printed in color. The more professional the booklet looks, the more it will please your advertisers and attract new customers.
* Research different options for online coupon booklets. You may want to go paperless, but a lot of people still prefer using coupons they can clip and hold in their hands.

INSPIRATION FROM KID ENTREPRENEURS JUST LIKE YOU!

NAME: Gary Kurek

TITLE: inventor

AGE: 19

WHERE: Alberta, Canada

WHAT: GET Mobility Solutions, Inc., which Gary founded when he was seventeen, helps people with health issues live independent lives.

HOW: Frustrated with the wheelchairs his grandmother had access to when she contracted a debilitating form of cancer, Gary invented a walker-wheelchair hybrid that responds to its own user's ever-changing levels of strength.

FUN FACT: Gary has also created a product that reduces motor vehicle collisions with wildlife and another that warns of avalanches.

RESOURCE: http://www.garykurek.com; www.getmobilityaids.com; http://thielfoundation.org/index.php?option=com_content&id=15

10

Curb Address Painter

*Numbers on curbs will mean numbers
in your bank account!*

You paint address numbers on the curb in front of houses. Customers will hire you to make their house easier to find by friends, service and delivery people, and emergency personnel.

SUPPLIES

You will need number stencils about six inches in height, dark-black indelible paint, and a paintbrush.

TIME NEEDED

Each address takes about fifteen minutes. You can paint the curbs of an entire neighborhood in one day!

WHAT TO CHARGE

$10 per house.

HOW TO ADVERTISE

When you ring doorbells, you might say: "Hello, my name is Kirby Painter, and I'd like to paint your house number on the curb. By having your address painted on the curb, visitors can find your house easily. The price is only $10, and I can have it done in fifteen minutes." If you are polite and convincing, many home-owners will accept your offer.

Another creative method of advertising would be to make a flyer that says: "Is it hard to see your address? Do visitors have trouble finding your house? It is important that friends and emergency personnel be able to locate your house quickly. For only $10, your address will be painted in large indelible black numbers on the curb by early tomorrow morning. Simply write a check payable to Martin Painter, note your address on this flyer, sign your name, put the check and this flyer in an envelope, and hang the envelope on your front doorknob. By noon tomorrow, your curb will be freshly painted." Distribute the flyers Friday afternoon. Return early Saturday morning and paint the numbers of those houses with envelopes on the doorknobs. To make extra money, you can distribute flyers to another neighborhood Saturday afternoon for painting Sunday morning.

You can make this a bigger business and start taking orders online from farther away in your city, but you really don't have to—this is a great small small business!

HINTS

* Most paints will last six months to a year. Check the neighbor-hoods frequently, and when the paint begins to wear off, try to sell your service again.
* When you go out to paint, wear old clothes. No matter how hard you try to stay clean, a little paint is bound to get on you!
* Buy your supplies at the paint store and specify exactly what you will be doing. Ask the owner for indelible black paint. Indelible paint is dangerous, so use caution while handling it.
* Before painting your first curb, practice many times on a sheet of paper. You don't want to make a mistake on a curb! If you do, paint over the address with a black rectangle. Let the paint dry and paint the numbers in indelible white paint over the black rectangle.

11

Disc Jockey (aka: DJ)

Spin the tunes, and party on!

You provide the music at parties, dances, and other events. You bring the equipment and the tunes. As a dj, you talk with guests and keep parties lively. If you enjoy entertaining and love music, this business is for you!

SUPPLIES

You don't need much beyond an mp3 player and speakers, a phone and advertising, and music, of course, but you can also buy or rent more elaborate turntables or stereo systems.

TIME NEEDED

The average party lasts about four hours. If you're working with basic equipment that you're familiar with, you will need about half an hour to set up before the event. Packing up will take about a half hour as well, because you should help the host tidy up after the party. Although cleanup is not your main duty as a disc jockey, it will please customers and possibly earn you a larger tip. This is generally weekend work, so be available Friday and Saturday evenings.

WHAT TO CHARGE

$25 per hour, including time to set up. If you have to travel a long distance, you may also charge for travel time and possibly the cost of a cab or other ride.

HOW TO ADVERTISE

Focus your advertising around holidays and summers, when people often have parties. Mention that you offer many kinds of music, including classic rock, country, classical, and pop. Pass the word around school that you can be hired as a dj. Visit student councils at schools in your area to sell your services for school dances.

HINTS

* Dress appropriately when you dj. If the function is formal, rent formal attire. At some parties, such as barbecues, you can wear jeans or other informal clothing appropriate to the theme of the party. Basically, you should dress as though you're attending the party as a guest.
* Keep in mind the rules around downloading music—just because you're downloading for your job doesn't mean you can ignore copyright law. If you need to buy a lot of music you wouldn't normally listen to for a particular party or client, consider asking the client to reimburse you for that. But also keep in mind: you may be able to use that music at someone else's event in the future!
* When you work, make your flyers available by placing them on a table. People at the party can pick one up if they like your service.
* In busy seasons, hire reliable friends to share the work with you. Split the money your friends collect. If you hire others to disc jockey at parties, call the customers after the events to be sure everything went well. Disc jockeys not only play music but

they keep parties going. To make a party more lively, circulate among guests and encourage them to participate in activities. If people are not dancing to one kind of music, try another. Take a request or two! Between songs, make humorous comments that entertain guests. Be sure your remarks are appropriate.

INSPIRATION FROM KID ENTREPRENEURS JUST LIKE YOU!

NAMES: Adam Holland and Jonathan Holland

TITLES: CEO and COO, respectively

AGES: 16 (Adam) and 15 (Jonathan)

WHERE: Washington, DC, USA

WHAT: Founders, owners, and the two who'll fill your order for a vicious vanilla or tiger's blood snow cone at AJ's Hawaiian Iceez, Adam and Jonathan truly put the A and the J in their company name.

HOW: All three of the Holland kids were accepted into elite schools, and they wanted to help their parents pay for their expensive educations. They and their friends love flavored shaved ice, so they decided that would be a fun and lucrative business idea. Their parents loaned them money for them to start AJ's, and they're paying it back with interest. Adam and Jonathan started their business in 2008, when they were just twelve and eleven years old, and last year they were able to fully pay for one year's tuition, even after they paid business costs. Adam and Jonathan were named 2011 Black Enterprise Teen Entrepreneurs of the Year.

FUN FACT: That z in their company name isn't for cute marketing purposes—it's for Zoe, their younger sister's name. (Isn't that just like older brothers, putting their little sister last?)

RESOURCE: www.ajsiceez.com

12

Document Preparer

There's no speed limit on words per minute!

Format and type basic Word documents for people who don't have the time, equipment, or skill to do the work themselves. Students and businesspeople will be your main clients.

SUPPLIES

You will need a phone, computer, and printer. A laser printer is best, if you have access to one. You should have advertising for your business. You have to be a quick and efficient typist to succeed at this business.

TIME NEEDED

Depending on how fast you type, it will take between five and fifteen minutes to type a page. The design and layout you are offering will be basic: making sure a memo looks nice on letterhead, aligning the columns in a table of data, inserting an image, and the like. Most people will send you many pages to be typed. Customers will often need documents immediately, so you need to be available to do urgent work.

WHAT TO CHARGE

$1.50 per page. If someone gives you a large order of twenty-five pages or more, charge $1 per page.

HOW TO ADVERTISE

If you live near a university, advertise in the student newspaper or in department e-newsletters. There are bulletin boards on campuses that allow free advertising. You can post several of your flyers. Universities are a good place to advertise, because students and professors often need papers and books typed.

Distribute flyers to local businesses whose owners may need typing services. Focus on small businesses that don't have administrative staff.

HINTS

* When customers send you written pages, call or email them to confirm that you received the papers. Tell them you will begin typing immediately. Be sure to ask what kind of format they want for the document and note their preferences on a checklist. For instance, find out if they need wide or narrow margins, single or double spacing, or paragraph indentations. When you finish, don't forget to proofread your work. Most clients will want their documents emailed back to them, which also automatically saves you a copy, but if they want them printed, make sure you save a copy on your computer. If the customer has given you paper originals to type, be particularly careful not to spill anything on the originals or otherwise damage them. Return them to the client along with the finished product, your bill, and five of your flyers so the customer can refer you to others.
* For customers who need papers typed quickly, offer to go to their houses or offices to pick up and deliver the work. Charge an additional fee for this service.

13

Dog Walker

You're barking up the right tree!

This business is great if you're a dog lover. You have the opportunity to enjoy animals and get paid at the same time!

SUPPLIES

You will need a phone or computer, a small shovel, plastic bags, and advertising.

TIME NEEDED

Plan on spending thirty minutes in the morning before school and thirty minutes in the evening. You can walk several dogs at once, but don't walk more than four at a time. You need to keep them under control!

WHAT TO CHARGE

$9 per trip per dog.

HOW TO ADVERTISE

Distribute flyers in your neighborhood. As a special touch, attach a dog biscuit to each flyer. You can walk around the neighborhood in the evening, introduce yourself, and give flyers to people you see walking dogs.

Put up posters advertising your service in apartment buildings and other housing complexes. Be sure to get permission first. Apartment complexes are excellent places to do business, because you can pick up many dogs at one location. This saves you time and energy.

Ask owners of local pet stores if you can leave flyers on their front desks. Tell them you will recommend their pet stores to your customers. When people come in to buy pet supplies, they will pick up one of your flyers.

HINTS

* Decide with your customers exactly when you will pick up the dog each day. This way you won't have to wait at houses for the owners to get their dogs ready. Eventually you'll have a complete schedule with few delays.

* In this business, you must be punctual. Customers are often on tight schedules and depend on you to show up at the designated time. You don't want your clients to be late for their appointments as a result of your tardiness!

* Be sure to learn the names of the dogs and always greet them with a kind word. For instance, say: "Good morning, Spike!" or "Good evening, Ralph!" Ask the owners the dates of their dogs' birthdays. Write them down and bring the dogs small presents on their birthdays. A bone or a squeaky toy will do the trick. These gestures will please dogs and, most important, impress owners.

* If you walk a dog often or walk a lot of dogs, you'll go through a lot of plastic bags—and that's hard on both the environment and your wallet. So price bags made of more Earth-friendly materials, or save and reuse the plastic bags you get from stores, that your newspaper comes in, and even the one that held your peanut butter and jelly sandwich for yesterday's lunch.

* When you walk the dogs, keep them on leashes and watch them carefully so they don't get into trouble! While you are with them, they are your responsibility.

* Most dogs will be friendly, but you may occasionally be asked to walk one that seems dangerous. It is better to refuse to walk a dangerous dog than to have one bite you.

INSPIRATION FROM KID ENTREPRENEURS JUST LIKE YOU!

NAME: Laura Deming

TITLE: entrepreneur

AGE: 17

WHERE: California, USA

WHAT: With her fund, IP Immortal, Laura plans on commercializing anti-aging research, with the goal of extending healthy lifespans, bringing therapies out of the lab and into the market sooner.

HOW: A determined spirit—and, of course, education, education, education. She started working in a biogerontology lab when she was twelve and was accepted into MIT at age fourteen. Laura also received a $100,000 fellowship to continue her work.

FUN FACT: Laura finds biology "beautiful" for many reasons, including this one: "It's 'real' magic. It's exhilarating to be at the bench, eyes glued to the microscope, and watch a tiny worm grow, and glow green, because of the genetic changes you've engineered. We get to manipulate invisible strands of information."

RESOURCE: http://laura-whatawonderfulworld.blogspot.com; http://thielfoundation.org/index.php?option=com_content&id=15

14

Dry Cleaning Deliverer

In this business, you can really clean up!

People often need clothes dry cleaned, but they don't have the time to deliver them to the cleaners and pick them up. You provide this service.

SUPPLIES

You will need a phone or computer, advertising, transportation to and from the dry cleaners, and a clipboard with paper. You will use the clipboard to record information about your customers.

TIME NEEDED

Be available to pick up dirty clothes from houses and clean clothes from the cleaners after school. Transporting clothes will take just a few minutes or a lot longer, depending on the distances between customers' houses, yours, and the dry cleaners.

WHAT TO CHARGE

$2 for the first article of clothing and $1 for each article after that. The customer pays for the dry cleaning.

HOW TO ADVERTISE

Distribute flyers to homes in your area. Your flyer might say: "Too busy to take your clothes to the dry cleaner? Let a hardworking kid help! Call Sue Tsarclean at 123-4567 or email Sue@email.com for fast and cheap pickup and delivery service." If you decide to knock on doors to advertise, emphasize that you will be available to pick up and deliver dry cleaning on a regular basis. Assure customers that you will handle their clothes with extreme care. Tell them that dresses and shirts will arrive without a wrinkle!

Ask the owner of a local dry cleaning shop if you can leave a stack of flyers on the front desk. Tell the owner that you will bring your customers' clothes to that shop if the owner agrees to pass out your flyers.

HINTS

* Before you start this business, find out what it costs to have shirts, blouses, suits, and other common items dry cleaned. Have a list of prices to show to your customers.

* When customers need dry cleaning, they call you. You go to their houses and pick up the clothes. You write down the customer's name, phone number, address, and quantity of each kind of clothing. Ask customers to sign the list, verifying what they have given you. Present the price list to the customer and explain that the amounts are approximate. Describe your fees. Collect the money for the approximate cleaning costs plus your fees, and promise to refund any money not charged by the cleaner. Say you will deliver the cleaning receipt with the clothes. Take the clothes to the cleaners, handling them carefully. As soon as the cleaning is done, return to the cleaners, get the clothes, and pay the costs. Deliver the clothes to the customer with one of your flyers attached.

* If you have a logo for your business and your business really takes off, consider printing yourself letterhead that you can write the clothing lists on. You'll be as impressive as the professionally cleaned clothes you're delivering!

15

Face Painter

Life can be all
rainbows and unicorns!

You paint pictures on children's faces at parties, fairs, carnivals, and other events, using special crayons or paints. Kids pick what they want. They love having their faces painted, so they'll beg their parents to pay for your services.

SUPPLIES

You will need advertising, a phone or a computer, a brightly colored outfit, a big sign, and special face crayons or paints. You can buy the materials at an art or party-supply store, or online. Be sure the crayons and paints are nontoxic and completely safe to use on faces. Check to see that they can be washed off with water. Although your drawings may be excellent, neither the children nor their parents will want them on their faces permanently!

TIME NEEDED

You work as much as you wish. You can choose to work an entire day or a few hours. If you pay for a permit to work at a fair, plan to stay the entire time it's open. The more hours you work, the more money you make.

WHAT TO CHARGE

$2 per face. To paint faces at carnivals and fairs, you might have to pay a fee to the carnival and fair organizers. If you do, be sure to charge each customer enough so that you make more money than what you paid the organizers.

HOW TO ADVERTISE

Dress colorfully when you're working. Have a big bright sign that advertises your services. Your sign might say: "Face painting here! Only $2 per design!" People will notice you! When children and their parents walk by, say to the children, "How would you like to have your face painted?" The children will beg their parents to have it done. The parents will give in, and you'll have a customer! When you're working, carry flyers and business cards, because someone might want to hire you for a birthday party or other occasion.

HINTS

* Paint your own face so people notice you while you work. To stand out, use many different colors. Paint your face as an animal, clown, mime, or other comic figure.

* There are other places where you can do face painting besides fairs and carnivals. Go to baseball and football games in your area. Die-hard fans might want the name of their favorite team painted on their faces. You can paint fans' faces as tigers, lions, crocodiles, Bengals, or other team mascots.

* Advertise two or three days before Halloween and offer face painting to go with children's costumes. On Halloween afternoon, sit in front of your house and wait for customers. Parents will bring their children to have their faces painted before the kids go trick-or-treating.

16

Flyer Distributor

Spread the word wide and far!

You distribute flyers in your neighborhood for local businesses that want to advertise. Small-business people have flyers printed and deliver them to your house. You circulate them to area houses and businesses.

SUPPLIES

You will need your own flyers—don't forget to advertise your business while you're advertising others'!—and a phone. You should have a backpack for carrying the customers' flyers. In the summer, you may want a water bottle, because you will get thirsty walking around the neighborhood. If houses are spread out in your area, you may need a bike or other form of transportation to deliver the flyers.

TIME NEEDED

One hundred flyers will take about two hours to distribute. You will have to spend time advertising your service to local small-business people.

WHAT TO CHARGE

$15 per one hundred flyers. If houses are spread out in your neighborhood, charge $20 per hundred flyers.

HOW TO ADVERTISE

Distribute your own flyers advertising your service to the small businesses in your area. Your flyer might say: "Fast and inexpensive flyer delivery to area homes and apartments. Dependable service by a hardworking kid. Call Dee Livery at 123-4567 or email Dee@email.com."

Introduce yourself to small-business people and describe your service. Tell owners you are energetic and efficient. Say you are willing to distribute flyers on quick notice if necessary. Emphasize that you guarantee delivery on the date specified. Ask local printing companies if you can advertise your business by leaving a stack of flyers on their front desks. Customers who use the print shop may pick up one of your flyers and call you.

HINTS

* Ask small-business people where they want you to put the flyers. For instance, you can throw them on the driveways, hang them from doorknobs, or attach them to newspapers early in the morning. Be careful about the newspaper method, because the newspaper company may not allow anything to be attached to the paper after delivery.
* Tell business owners you'll distribute their flyers for $13 per hundred instead of $15 if they are willing to have "Distributed by (your name and phone number/email)" printed in small letters in the bottom right corner of the flyers. You get free advertising, because the people who receive the flyer will read your name and phone number.
* As an additional service, you can offer to give a small sales pitch about your customers' businesses to homeowners when you distribute the flyers. Charge $45 per one hundred flyers for this service, because it will take you much longer and require more of your skills.

INSPIRATION FROM KID ENTREPRENEURS JUST LIKE YOU!

NAME: Leanna Archer

TITLE: CEO, motivational speaker, philanthropist

AGE: 15

WHERE: New York, USA

WHAT: Leanna founded and runs Leanna's, Inc., which makes organic hair care products using her grandmother's family recipes. The formulas are free of sodium lauryl sulfate and parabens, unhealthy and dangerous chemicals. She's a regular speaker at youth empowerment conferences, and in 2008 she founded the Leanna Archer Education Foundation, which works toward better educational opportunities for kids in Haiti.

HOW: A product's best promoter is someone who uses that product—and Leanna was her own first customer. At age nine, she got the idea for her business because she kept receiving compliments on her own hair.

FUN FACT: Leanna's, Inc., hires kid representatives to help sell the products across the country.

RESOURCE: www.leannashair.com

17

Fresh-Flower Deliverer

While your customers enjoy the sweet smell of flowers, you'll enjoy the sweet smell of success!

By the weekends, many people like to have fresh flowers in their homes, but they don't have time to buy them during the week. You deliver fresh flowers to homes in your area on Thursday or Friday nights or Saturday mornings. Customers agree to have you bring flowers every weekend.

SUPPLIES

You will need a phone or computer, business cards, a strong pair of scissors, and large sheets of paper. You will use the scissors to trim the flowers and the large sheets of paper to wrap them. Some vendors from which you buy the flowers will do this for you—bonus!

TIME NEEDED

Once you have a set group of customers, this entire business can be run Saturday morning (or Thursday or Friday after school—some of your clients may be interested in having fresh flowers before their full weekend entertaining starts). You will need to buy flowers from the florist early, so you have time to arrange them. Don't buy them until the afternoon or morning of the delivery. Delivering the flowers will take between three and ten minutes per house, depending on how close your customers' houses are to each other.

WHAT TO CHARGE

$15 per delivery. You must be careful not to spend more than $10 on flowers per visit per customer, because you need to make a profit. Four dollars will not buy many flowers, so try to find a florist who will give you a discount.

HOW TO ADVERTISE

Have business cards made with your name, service, and contact information on them. On a Saturday morning, go to a florist and buy some inexpensive flowers. Visit houses in your neighborhood. Describe your service to homeowners and give out a flower and your business card. If homeowners express interest, collect the first month's fee immediately!

HINTS

* You arrange with a florist in your area to buy flowers on every week. As you will be a regular customer, try to get the florist to give you a special discount. Buy the flowers from the florist each week. Go back to your house and arrange them in separate bouquets for each customer. Deliver the flowers and collect your money!

* Customers may not want to receive the same arrangement every Saturday. Try to vary the colors and types of flowers you deliver. Around certain holidays, you may want to choose special colors. For instance, before Halloween you can use near-black and orange flowers to make your arrangements. Put one of your business cards in every bouquet that you deliver. Your customers will remember the name of your service and recommend it to their friends.

18

Garbage Can Mover

*It's a dirty business, but someone's
got to make money doing it!*

You take customers' garbage cans out to the street before garbage day. You bring the cans back to the customers' houses
after garbage day. Many people forget to put out their garbage
or don't have time to do it. Yes, you have to "take the garbage
out" often, but you get paid for it!

SUPPLIES

You will need warm clothes if you live in a climate that gets cold
during the winter. In all weather, you'll want gloves to keep your
hands clean.

TIME NEEDED

It will take about thirty seconds to put out a customer's garbage
can. Bringing it in will take thirty seconds more. Allow time to
go between customers' houses.

WHAT TO CHARGE

$16 per month. Collect your fee at the beginning of the month, before you do the service.

HOW TO ADVERTISE

Use the door-to-door advertising method. To be entertaining as you advertise, pull your garbage can around to each house in your neighborhood. When someone comes to the door, you might say: "Hello, my name is Rhea Lee Gross. Do you despise taking the garbage can out and bringing it back in? For only $16 per month, I'll do your garbage chores for you." People might pay you the first $16 right on the spot, and you can start immediately!

If people aren't home, leave a flyer for them. Your flyer might say: "Dislike taking out the garbage? Hate the smell, dirt, and grime? A reliable kid will take out your garbage can and bring it back in for a small fee. Call Rhea Lee Gross at 123-4567 or email Rhea@email.com."

HINTS

* You can offer another service related to this business. On the day you take the garbage can to the street, before you do so, you go through the house and empty the trash containers into plastic bags. You empty ashtrays, litter boxes, and other indoor trash bins. After you've done the street work for several months, ask your customers if they would like you to do this extra service. Charge $8 per month more for the inside trash service.
* Still another service related to garbage is washing customers' garbage cans. Pick a sunny day and ask your customers if they wish to have their inside and outside cans washed. If so, use their garden hose and liquid soap. To remove gum and other trash stuck to the cans, use a putty knife or long spatula. This is messy work, so you can charge between $1 and $5 per can, depending on the size.

* You may not be able to put the cans out right before the garbage collectors arrive. For example, if they arrive very early
in the morning, and you can't get a ride to that neighborhood
that early, you may have to talk with your customers about taking the bins out the night before. Then you'll have to return
the next day to pull the bins in. This is a good reason to stick
to your immediate neighborhood. You don't want to miss the
garbage collectors and cause your clients to have to live with
overflowing bins an extra week!

* You need to have many customers to make money in this
business. If you're reliable, you shouldn't have trouble getting
clients. Go around the neighborhood every month or so and
offer the service again to the people who initially rejected your
offer. Eventually, they might hire you.

19

Gift-Basket Maker

Weave through obstacles
on your way to success!

You produce gift baskets and send them wherever customers wish. You offer a list of themes from which they can select. Customers choose the price of the basket they want to send. The baskets you produce contain nonperishable foods and treats such as jellies, jams, mustard, crackers, olives, other canned and bottled goods, small toys and games, candy, or fun notecards.

SUPPLIES

You will need a phone or computer, large sheets of cellophane wrap, many colors of string or ribbon, tissue paper in a variety of colors, beautiful and fun baskets, big boxes, and paper or Styrofoam pieces to pack the baskets in the boxes. Most of all, you need to have a great imagination!

TIME NEEDED

One hour will be required to shop for the contents of each basket. Once you have had practice, assembling a basket will take about a half hour.

WHAT TO CHARGE

Have different price categories for the baskets. For instance, offer $25, $45, $65, and $90 versions. The more expensive the basket, the more products you put in it. Try not to spend more than half of what you charge the customer on supplies and postage. For example, if a customer orders a $45 version, try not to spend more than $22.50 on supplies and postage. Your profit is the other half of the price, or $22.50!

HOW TO ADVERTISE

Around holidays, distribute your flyers to businesses in your area. Companies often like to send gift baskets to clients at special times of the year. Emphasize that you can send baskets anywhere in the world. This is a business that you can advertise and take orders for as well online as you can in person.

HINTS

* Design creative baskets according to popular themes. For example, a golf basket might include candy golf balls, real golf balls, crackers, can insulators, and golf tees. A cat theme might contain a calendar with pictures of cats, a ball of pretty yarn, cat treats, catnip seeds and a pretty pot, and cans of fine tuna. A football theme might have a football, football handbook, potato chips, a can of pop, and several TV guides with football games highlighted in yellow! Get the idea?

* You should be able to find a shop near you or online that sells inexpensive woven baskets. Locate another store that sells high-quality but reasonably priced jams, mustards, crackers, olives, and similar specialty products. Import stores are often best for these items.

* When you pack the basket for sending, be careful to arrange the contents so they don't get smashed or damaged. Avoid using glass containers.

INSPIRATION FROM KID ENTREPRENEURS JUST LIKE YOU!

NAME: Eden Full

TITLE: inventor

AGE: 19

WHERE: New Jersey and California, USA; Alberta, Canada

WHAT: The SunSaluter, a solar panel that rotates without electricity and is cheaper and requires less maintenance than traditional solar systems, is an innovation Eden is working on through her Roseicollis Technologies, a company she started at age fifteen.

HOW: Eden is one of the first young people to win a 20 Under 20 Fellowship from the Thiel Foundation. In order to accept the $100,000 award, Eden had to follow the fellowship's unconventional rule: She had to leave college for two years to focus on her invention. All fellows must put on hold for two years what they were doing at the time of the award to use the award.

FUN FACT: When asked by her school, Princeton University, to "describe your 8-year-old self in 5 words or less," she answered, "I love Pokemon."

RESOURCE: www.universitypressclub.com/archive/2011/05/21-questions-with-eden-full-13; www.businessweek.com/technology/content/may2011/tc20110524_317819.htm; http://thielfoundation.org/index.php?option=com_content&id=15

20

Gift Wrapper

Tie it up with a ribbon on top!

You box, wrap, and send gifts for people before the holidays. People drop the gifts off at your home, or you set up a stand in a local shopping mall.

SUPPLIES

You will need a phone or computer, advertising, a postage scale, wrapping paper, boxes, colored ribbon, string, tape, and other packaging supplies. Buy wrapping paper after each holiday season, when it's on sale, and save it for the next year.

TIME NEEDED

You will be busiest during holiday seasons. If you open a stand at a mall, plan to work evenings and weekends. Holiday times are hectic, but they offer you the chance to make money!

If you run the business out of your home, customers will drop off gifts often during the weeks leading up to the holiday. Each gift takes about five minutes to wrap. If customers want you to send gifts, allow time to go to the post office.

WHAT TO CHARGE

$5 per gift if you only wrap it, and $10 if you wrap and send it. If the customer wants you to send the gift, figure out the cost of postage using the postage scale and add it to your fee.

HOW TO ADVERTISE

If you plan to run the business from your home, distribute flyers in your neighborhood about three and a half weeks before a holiday. In the flyers, describe your service and list your contact information. When people call or email you, remind them to affix a personalized card to each gift, if they wish. Definitely have them attach a note that indicates the age, sex, name, and address of the receiver of the gift. You will custom-wrap the gifts according to the age and sex of the receivers. Arrange a time for the customer to drop off the gifts at your house.

If you're setting up a stand in a shopping mall, check with mall management about any rules they have and, if allowed, give stores your flyers to post near their front desks. Mall customers will buy gifts in the stores, and they'll come to you to get them wrapped. Put up a big poster near your stand, so people walking by will know the service you offer. Wrap several empty boxes with the different wrapping papers available to customers. Display the samples near your stand, so customers can choose the wrapping style they like best.

HINTS

* The winter holidays are not the only time you can run this business. You can wrap gifts before Mother's Day, Father's Day, Grandparents' Day, and other holidays when people exchange gifts.
* You can have business cards printed that might say: "Gift wrapped by Sara N. Wrap. Call 123-4567 or email Sarah@ email.com." Attach a business card to each gift you wrap, and you'll get more customers.

21

Grocery Deliverer

*Fresh food from the store
to your customer's door.*

You buy and deliver groceries for people who don't have time or aren't able to shop. A family with working parents will rely on your service. An elderly person who can't leave the house will call on you.

SUPPLIES

You will need a supermarket within bike-riding distance of your house, a bike, two bike baskets to carry the groceries or a cart to pull them, the proper bike-safety equipment, and advertising.

TIME NEEDED

Whenever possible, establish a regular schedule with customers, but you can decide to be open for last-minute orders, too. Each grocery delivery will take between thirty minutes and one hour, depending on the number and type of products the customer wants you to purchase.

WHAT TO CHARGE

$8 for the first bag of groceries, and $3 for each additional one. This is what you earn, and the customer, not you, pays for the groceries.

HOW TO ADVERTISE

Distribute flyers in your area about once a month. Say in your flyer that you do general grocery delivery. Indicate that you also offer immediate product shopping and delivery for parties.

Go door-to-door to advertise your business. When people answer, describe your services. If customers need convincing, offer to do the first delivery free. Ask them if they need something right away. If they take you up on your offer for a free first service, leave five flyers in the grocery bag when you deliver it.

Advertise at local businesses, too—people need food delivered for business lunch meetings and after-work events.

This is a good service to advertise and take orders for online!

HINTS

* When someone calls you, ask them for their name, address, and directions to the delivery site. Tell them you will come quickly. Ask them to make a list of the products needed, including preferred brands or sizes, if possible. When you arrive at the house, look over the list to make sure you understand the names of the products. Check that no alcohol is on the list, because kids can't purchase it. Estimate the cost of each product and add up the total. Then add a standard cushion, so you don't run out of money at the register. For example, if you figure the cost at the supermarket will be $10, ask the customer for $15. Go to the supermarket, buy the items, and be sure to get a receipt. When you return to the customer, present the receipt, explain how much you paid for the items, give the customer the change, and request your fee.

* Some of your customers may be extremely busy or unable to leave the house, and they will use your services frequently. Be especially attentive to these clients, because they will bring you repeat business.

22

Homework Helper

Practice makes perfect.

You help children who are having trouble with their homework by providing an after-school and weekend tutoring service. You assist kids in math, science, history, social studies, reading, English, and other subjects that may be difficult.

SUPPLIES

You will need a phone or computer, advertising, and lots of patience. Teaching is not an easy business, so try to be understanding with the kids you tutor, particularly when they don't after the first—or even after the second or the third—time learn what you are teaching them. Be understanding with yourself, too. You're a good tutor, and you too are learning when you're teaching.

TIME NEEDED

This depends on how many customers you have on a certain afternoon. The average child will need one hour of tutoring per session. For example, if you have five customers on a given day, you will need to set aside five hours. Don't neglect your own homework, friends, and family—such long hours may work on weekend days only.

WHAT TO CHARGE

$8 per hour. If you help more than one child at the same time, charge the parents $6 per extra child per hour.

HOW TO ADVERTISE

Knock on doors in your neighborhood, explain your service to parents, and give out flyers.

Place a small advertisement in the bulletins or newsletters of the elementary schools in your area. Your ad might say: "Is your child frustrated with a subject at school? If so, call I. B. Smart, a responsible student, at 123-4567 or email IB@email.com for excellent tutoring." Consider putting your age and grade level in the advertisement, if space permits.

Visit teachers at local elementary schools. Ask them to distribute flyers to the parents of students who are struggling in certain subjects.

HINTS

* Always be polite when you talk to parents. Remember, the parents, not the kids, are paying you. Take a personal interest in your students and remember the problems they're having. For instance, when you arrive at a child's house, say, "So, how did you do on the test we studied for?" Parents will appreciate the special attention you give to their children.
* You may want to research online or check out books at a local library in order to learn teaching methods. There are several basic guidelines to follow. Figure out the problem the child is having in school. After you explain the lesson, have the student practice the skill. Correct what the student has practiced. Don't be critical if the student doesn't understand. Always find something positive to say. If you make students feel good, they'll improve in class and ask their parents to have you back.
* Give your students a small treat, like a piece of candy, after each study session, and you will be a hit. (Get parents' approval for the treat beforehand.) Before each holiday, bring your students small gifts or share other tokens of appreciation.

INSPIRATION FROM KID ENTREPRENEURS JUST LIKE YOU!

NAME: Savannah Britt

TITLE: writer, editor-in-chief, publisher

AGE: 17

WHERE: New Jersey, USA

WHAT: As the founder and editor-in-chief of Girlpez Fashion Magazine, which has offered both print and online issues, Savannah is a true mover and shaker, interviewing celebrities and attending fashion shows and philanthropic events.

HOW: Savannah has been a writer for a long time, publishing her first poem at age eight and working as a paid book reviewer for a newspaper with a readership of 70,000. Her parents have served as role models in publishing and in general organization and management skills and offer guidance when Savannah feels overwhelmed—which can happen when you're balancing honors classes, basketball practice, and your own business, as Savannah is.

FUN FACT: One of Savannah's passions is hip-hop and she'd like to host a conference for kids in the industry to discuss the way genders and races are portrayed in hip-hop songs, videos, and ads.

RESOURCE: www.girlpez.com

23

House Checker

Keep an eye out!

While people are on vacation, you check on and take care of their houses. You bring in the mail and newspaper every day and pile them neatly inside the house. Customers who own plants will want you to water them. People with animals may ask you to walk and feed them several times a day.

SUPPLIES

You will need a flashlight, key ring, small labels, phone, and advertising. When you enter houses at night, the flashlight will be handy. Use the key ring to keep the keys of your customers' homes, so you won't lose them. Attach a label to each key to identify the house to which it belongs.

TIME NEEDED

Time will vary according to the number of visits a day each customer requests. Count on fifteen minutes per visit. If you go on vacation over the major holidays, this business may not be suited for you. You need to be home during holiday seasons, because that's when people go away and need you to care for their houses.

WHAT TO CHARGE

$5 per visit to check on the house, and $10 per visit to check on the house and care for pets.

HOW TO ADVERTISE

Four weeks before major holidays, distribute flyers to houses in your area. If you distribute flyers too far in advance of vacation, people might throw them away.

Knock on doors, introduce yourself, and explain your service to people in your neighborhood. Tell them you are reliable and will take excellent care of their homes and pets. Assure them that all will be well when they return.

Referrals from past satisfied customers work as particularly good advertising in this business!

HINTS

* If the customer wants you to visit the house twice daily, you should turn the outside lights on at night and off in the morning. This makes the house look lived in. If the customer is away for more than five days, you may need to water plants both inside and outside. Ask the customer if you can provide other services.

* To be organized, make a checklist of the services you offer and fill one out for each customer. Be sure to ask customers for phone numbers where they can be reached in case of emergency. Have customers sign the bottom of the checklist, showing that they agree to have you care for their home. If a police officer or neighbor asks why you are in someone else's home, you can explain by showing the signed checklist.

* Write "Welcome home!" on one of your flyers and leave it with two or three fresh flowers on the kitchen table when you make your last visit to the house. This pleases customers and encourages them to use your service again.

* Try not to visit houses after dark. If you must, ask one of your parents to come along.

INSPIRATION FROM KID ENTREPRENEURS JUST LIKE YOU!

NAME: Katherine Commale

TITLE: activist, fund-raiser

AGE: 10

WHERE: Pennsylvania, USA

WHAT: According to the PBS program *Malaria: Fever Wars*, malaria kills two children every minute, but the disease is mostly preventable—if only every bed in Africa was draped with a bed net to keep out malaria-carrying mosquitos.

HOW: At age five, Katherine joined her mother in raising funds to buy insecticide-treated bed nets for people in Africa, to prevent the spread of malaria. Together, they made their first presentation to their church, making particular effort to involve the kids. Later that year, Katherine led kids in decorating gift certificates, allowing gift givers to purchase bed nets in their friends' names. They raised more than $10,000 and were invited to the launch of Nothing But Nets, a major bed-net nonprofit. Katherine and her mother continue to represent the cause in national media and local presentations and raise funds through their Nothing But Nets fund-raising team, One Bed Net at a Time.

FUN FACT: You don't have to start your organization to make a big difference—Katherine's passion and efforts help Nothing But Nets succeed.

RESOURCE: www.nothingbutnets.net/partners-people/champions/lynda-katherine.html; www.globalproblems-globalsolutions.org/site/TR/Events/NBN?team_id=1040&pg=team&fr_id=1040

24

Jewelry Maker

Sparkle and shine,
trendy, casual, or fine!

You make necklaces, earrings, bracelets, pins, and other jewelry using beads, thread, and other materials you buy or find. You sell your jewelry at craft and art fairs. If your jewelry is creative, you may be able to sell it to stores in your area.

SUPPLIES

You will need a phone or computer, work table, and the materials to make your jewelry. If you plan to sell your work at fairs, you'll need poster board and markers to make signs.

TIME NEEDED

Making the jewelry will take from a few minutes to several hours per item, depending on your skill and the quality of the jewelry. Plan to spend several afternoons visiting stores in your area to sell your work. If you sell at a craft or art fair, set aside an entire day. You know already how much time the internet can suck away from you, but jewelry is a great product to sell online, via your website and in virtual arts and crafts markets.

WHAT TO CHARGE

Jewelry can be sold at a high markup. This means you can sell it for a lot more than you paid for supplies. Sell each piece for at least twice the cost of supplies. If you pay $5 for beads, string, and a clasp to make a necklace, charge $10 for it. If you sell to stores in your area, expect to have to lower the prices a bit, because stores must resell the merchandise to make a profit. Most stores will have set terms for taking product on consignment.

HOW TO ADVERTISE

At craft and art fairs, make attractive signs to post near your booth. To sell to stores in your area, offer to give them two pieces of jewelry free. If the jewelry sells, the store owners will call you and buy more.

HINTS

* Watch for announcements of craft shows and art fairs in your area. Figure your costs carefully before you rent a table or booth, because you will usually have to pay for it before the show. Be sure you can make enough money at the fair to cover your costs. Some fairs will allow anyone to rent space, but others will allow only professional artists to display their work. Don't be discouraged if a few shows won't allow you to rent a table or booth, because many will.

* Be creative in your jewelry design and make it as unique as possible. To get you started, here are a few suggestions: Make pins and earrings out of recycled materials, such as bottle caps, pieces of pop cans, and newspaper scraps. Use old microchips to make contemporary necklaces and earrings. Take them out of broken toys or call a local used-computer store to request them. Look around your room for things you might otherwise want to sell or give away—could you take apart any of them and use some of their parts for jewelry? Now think of other ideas!

* Some stores will prefer to carry your jewelry on consignment. In a consignment agreement, the stores pay you only when the merchandise sells. Business owners don't have to take a risk by buying your jewelry outright. If a store can't sell the merchandise, the owner will return it to you, because you still own it.

25

Landscaper

As you plant customers' flowers, you'll be growing your own money tree!

You make dull, brown yards look colorful and bright by planting flowers. You choose, purchase, plant, and water flowers for customers in your neighborhood.

SUPPLIES

You will need a phone or computer, advertising, and planting tools. You probably can find a shovel, hoe, and other tools around your house. If you can't, buy them at a garage sale, because they will be expensive at a hardware store. Buy the flowers from a nursery offering them on sale.

TIME NEEDED

Planting flowers in a customer's yard can take an entire day. Planting a small flower box or garden will take a few hours. Allow at least an hour to visit the nursery to choose the flowers.

WHAT TO CHARGE

$7.25 per hour that you plant flowers. If you buy plants and soil, charge the customer for the cost of these supplies. Offer to water the flowers every other day, and charge $1 per visit for this service.

HOW TO ADVERTISE

Knock on doors in your neighborhood and introduce yourself. Explain your service and hand out flyers. You can offer to plant a free flower to show the homeowner the quality of your work.

If you choose to distribute flyers to houses without contacting homeowners, attach a flower to each flyer and leave it on the doorstep. Homeowners will be impressed by the thought, and they surely won't throw out the flyer.

After you have decorated a few gardens, take pictures of your best work. You can have the pictures enlarged to impress potential clients, and don't forget to create a beautiful slideshow of images on your website (it's easy to do and looks impressive!).

Once you have several satisfied customers, get letters of recommendation detailing the quality of your work. You can show the letters to homeowners unsure about hiring you.

HINTS

* If you don't know much about the landscape business, research online or go to your local library and check out books on the topic. Look for websites and books that focus on flower design and plant maintenance. Learn the names of the most popular flowers, so you can be knowledgeable about your business.

* Once you have customers who like your work, you can expand your business to include landscape maintenance. You can offer bush trimming, leaf raking, and lawn mowing.

* When you work, always wear old clothes, and in summer bring something to drink, because you may get thirsty. Your flowers will get thirsty too, so don't forget to water them immediately after planting them. When you're finished planting, be sure to offer your plant-watering service to the homeowner.

INSPIRATION FROM KID ENTREPRENEURS JUST LIKE YOU!

NAME: Cecilia Cassini

TITLE: fashion designer

AGE: 11

WHERE: California, USA

WHAT: Currently designing and making dresses decorated with lots of ruffles and bows, Cecilia sells her creations online and in stores in Southern California.

HOW: Ever since she could wield a pair of scissors (four years old), Cecilia has been cutting up and . . . let's call it *repurposing* her and her family's clothes. She held the new garments in place with hairbands until she received a sewing machine for her sixth birthday. While her classmates take a break at recess, she gets ahead in her homework. That way she can sew after school and mentor other kids to follow their dreams now—and occasionally hobnob with her celebrity fans at Hollywood events. She makes about one hundred one-of-a-kind handmade pieces a year.

FUN FACT: A portion of every purchase goes to Children's Hospital Los Angeles.

RESOURCE: www.ceciliacassini.com

26

Leaf Raker

Sweep away the colors of autumn.

People love to look at fall colors but hate to do yard cleanup. You rake and bag leaves for customers during the fall season.

SUPPLIES

You will need advertising, a phone or computer, a rake, and a compost can, and bags. A plastic rake is lighter and easier to use than a metal one. Your clients will probably want you to use the compost bin they put at the curb, but you might need to bring bags for overflow leaves. And if they want you to put the leaves in their backyard compost pile, instead of in a bin on wheels, you might want to rake the leaves into bags or a cart, which you can then carry to the backyard. You don't want to waste time making small trips transferring leaves or changing small bags often.

TIME NEEDED

To rake leaves on most properties, you will need about three hours. If there is snow or frost on the ground, the work will take longer. Set aside afternoon time, since it may be too cold to work in the mornings or evenings.

WHAT TO CHARGE

$7.25 per hour. Certain customers may prefer to receive a fixed price for the work. In this case, try to estimate how many hours you will work and multiply by your $7.25-per-hour fee.

HOW TO ADVERTISE

Before leaves begin to fall, distribute flyers to the houses in your area. Your flyers might say: "Enjoy the spectacle of fall without doing the cleanup. Let a hardworking kid rake and bag your leaves for a small fee. Call Lee F. Raker at 123-4567 or email Lee@ email.com." Staple a leaf to each flyer to make the advertisement more attractive, or cut your flyer into a leaf shape or print it on orange or gold paper.

Instead of leaving flyers, you may want to knock on doors and introduce yourself. When you visit houses, carry a bag full of leaves and a rake. You might say: "Hi. Soon you'll have to spend three or four hours to rake and bag the leaves on your property. I'll do it for only $7.25 an hour." Point to the lawn and the bag of leaves you're carrying and add, "I'll pack up those leaves like this!"

If you see neighbors raking leaves, run over and offer to relieve them of the chore. Tell them you'll finish the work, so they can go inside and relax! You can even offer to do that little bit of work as your complimentary trial job.

HINTS

* There is an easy way to gather leaves. Rake leaves into piles. Scoop the piles of leaves into the bag using the rake and one arm. When the bag is full, tie it up and replace it. If you're going old-school and using bushel-size plastic bags, put the plastic bag in a trash can first, even if you're going to put the bag on the curb alone. Using the garbage can as a container is easier than scooping leaves straight into the bag.
* Make a large stand-up sign. On the sign, write: "Lee F. Raker is raking leaves here. To have your leaves raked, call 123-4567 or email Lee@email.com." Place the sign near the street while you are working. People driving by will see it and call you.
* Keep an eye on your customers' lawns. When leaves begin to gather, visit the house and offer to rake again.

27

Muffin and Juice Deliverer

Cracking eggs at the crack of dawn!

People love fresh breakfast foods but don't have the time to prepare them. You bake muffins and squeeze fresh juice for Saturday delivery to your customers. Some people will want muffins, others juice, and some may request both.

SUPPLIES

You will need advertisements and a phone or a computer. To bake muffins, you will need an oven, muffin pans, and whatever food ingredients are necessary. To squeeze fresh juice, you will need a juicer and fruit. An electric juicer will save you time and energy, so try to find one around the house or buy one cheaply.

TIME NEEDED

Preparation and delivery time will depend on how many customers you have. To bake a dozen muffins takes about an hour. To squeeze one bottle of fresh juice takes about thirty minutes. Depending on the distance of your customers' houses from each other, allow between five and fifteen minutes per house for delivery.

WHAT TO CHARGE

Charge monthly, and collect your fee at the beginning of each month before you deliver the goods. Charge $30 per month for one dozen muffins delivered every Saturday. Charge $20 per month for one bottle of fresh juice delivered every Saturday. Offer your customers a special price of $45 per month for muffins and juice. Remind potential customers that muffins and juice in a supermarket or at a coffee shop will cost more than the price you offer.

HOW TO ADVERTISE

Knock on doors and offer a sample muffin or a cup of fresh juice. Describe your service to potential customers and hand out flyers. When homeowners answer the door, you might say: "Hi, I'm Muff N. Bringer. I bake muffins and squeeze fresh juice for people in the neighborhood. I deliver the food every Saturday morning, and I guarantee it will be fresh. My prices are much less than what you'd spend in the market or at a restaurant. You won't have to leave home, and the muffins and juice will be freshly prepared. Would you like to try a sample?"

HINTS

* Have a print shop make stickers with the name of your business and phone number on them. Put a sticker on every bag of muffins and bottle of juice you deliver. Customers will be reminded of your business, so they can easily refer you to others.
* Bake theme foods around the holidays. For instance, top your muffins with orange frosting at Halloween, or draw turkeys with frosting on the tops of your muffins at Thanksgiving.
* Though customers interested in this service will enjoy the surprise of different muffins each week, you should ask for some guidance from each new client. You don't want to make a whole batch of cinnamon walnut muffins for someone who hates cinnamon and is allergic to nuts.

* During certain seasons and in some areas, supplies such as oranges may cost more than you expect. If so, be sure to raise your prices enough so that you still make a profit for yourself.

INSPIRATION FROM KID
ENTREPRENEURS JUST LIKE YOU!

NAME: Alec Loorz

TITLE: nonprofit founder, speaker

AGE: 16

WHERE: California, USA

WHAT: Kids vs Global Warming teaches environmental science and advocacy to kids in kindergarten through college.

HOW: Motivated by Al Gore's movie *An Inconvenient Truth*, Alec founded Kids vs Global Warming to share the message that young people can make a difference in the transition away from fossil fuels. His energetic and thoughtful presentations caught Gore's attention, and Alec became the youngest trained presenter for the Climate Project. His organization coordinated youth marches, called "iMatter," in 43 countries and 160 cities to let society know that their future matters.

FUN FACT: There's an app for that—iMatter, which grew out of Kids vs Global Warming, connects different kids' environmental actions to make one global impact.

RESOURCE: iMatterYouth.org

28

Mural Painter

For an artist,
the wall is a canvas.

You paint colorful murals in doctors' offices, schools, pre-schools, day-care centers, and children's bedrooms. Popular themes will include animals, sports, and nature. You must be an excellent artist if you are to make this venture successful.

SUPPLIES

You will need a phone and computer, advertising, painting supplies, and old clothes. For most walls, indoor latex paint will work best. It dries quickly, doesn't leave an odor, and can be washed off your hands with soap and water. Drop cloths are essential, because you need to protect customers' floors and furniture. Be sure to wear old clothes, because part of the mural may end up on you!

TIME NEEDED

Painting a mural will take between five and thirty hours, depending on the size. For large murals, you'll have to return to the location several times to finish the painting.

WHAT TO CHARGE

Before you tell the customer the price, find out how much the paint supplies will cost. Depending on the size of the mural, charge between $10 and $100 more than the cost of your supplies.

Some customers will want to pay you by the hour instead of by the mural. Charge $15 per hour for your work plus the cost of supplies. Show the customer your receipts.

HOW TO ADVERTISE

Draw an attractive flyer and distribute it to offices of pediatricians, school principals, preschools, and day-care centers. You can do door-to-door advertising and show parents sample designs for murals for their children's rooms. You might say: "Hi, I'm Mirielle

Painter. Would you like to give your children the gift of a wall mural for the holidays? Here are sample sketches of designs."

When you finish a mural, write your name and contact information in small letters in the bottom right corner. People who see the mural will call you if they want one!

And don't forget to take photos of your work to post online!

HINTS

* Use shirt paints to put your name and contact information on the front and back of a T-shirt. Wear the shirt when you're working. While you're painting a mural, people who pass by will learn your name and information.

* Before you start painting a mural, decide with customers exactly what they want on the wall. Sketch out the design as many times as necessary until your customers are satisfied. Once you start painting, you can't erase anything!

* Be careful not to splatter paint on your customers' furniture and floors. Put drop cloths over everything.

29

New-Product Assembler

Putting it all together, piece-by-piece!

You assemble new products for people who don't have the time or the know-how. You put together bikes, hook up stereos, set up computers, and construct swing sets.

SUPPLIES

You will need a phone or computer, tool kit, and advertising. The tool kit should include hammer, wrench, pliers, ruler, variety of screwdrivers, and other basic tools. If you don't have tools at home, look for them at garage sales or online, where they will be cheap.

TIME NEEDED

Depending on the size of the product, assembly time will range from one to eight hours.

WHAT TO CHARGE

You can charge by the number of hours you work or by the product you assemble. If you charge by the hour, ask $7.25 per hour. If you charge by the item, prices will vary. For example, bikes might cost $25, stereos $30, computers $35, and swing sets $45.

When you consider your fees, find out how much stores charge to assemble the products, and make your prices a little bit lower.

HOW TO ADVERTISE

Ask the owners of bike shops, appliance stores, and swing-set companies to give your flyers to purchasers of unassembled products. To create an incentive for the owner to help, offer to assemble one of the store's floor models for every referral you get. When customers call, ask them which store referred them to you.

Distribute flyers to houses in your neighborhood. On the top of the flyer, draw the parts of an unassembled bicycle. On the rest of the page, you might write: "Do you have trouble assembling products? Don't struggle any more putting together bikes, appliances, computers, swing sets, and other products. Call Manny Parts at 123-4567 or email Manny@email.com for inexpensive quality assembly by a hardworking kid."

You could do some clever advertising by making and posting how-to videos online—but don't give away too many of your fix-it tips!

HINTS

* In a customer's house, always put down paper bags, newspapers, or drop cloths on which to work, so you don't damage the floor or carpet. Be careful of oils and grease, because they can stain carpets permanently.
* Leave the extra pieces you don't use, such as leftover screws and bolts, with your customers. They may need them later.
* Bring a stapler and staple one of your flyers to the warranty papers and instructions that come with the products. When customers need additional work and refer to the papers, they will find your flyer and call you. Leave five extra flyers with each customer, so they can give them to friends.
* Before assembling a product, read the instructions carefully. Note dangerous steps and be especially careful when doing

them. Make sure the product has all necessary parts before you begin. Since you'll probably know what make and model product you'll be assembling before the job, look that product up online before your appointment with your client. Many manuals are available online, so with a little preparation, you can really show your stuff to the customer.

* If your business gets big, you can pay a local print shop to make small stickers with your name and phone number on them. When you assemble a product, put one of your stickers on it.

INSPIRATION FROM KID ENTREPRENEURS JUST LIKE YOU!

NAME: Laurence Rook

TITLE: inventor

AGE: 13

WHERE: Great Britain

WHAT: Laurence's Smart Bell is a doorbell designed to trick would-be burglars into believing someone's at home—when really, no one is. When pressed, the bell calls the homeowner's cell phone, allowing them to talk to the person at the door, even if the owner is buying milk at the grocery store or in line for a roller coaster thousands of miles away. This can be useful even for friendly visitors: homeowners could tell delivery people where to safely leave packages or remind friends of their trip. Within a year of developing Smart Bell, Laurence has his product in four major stores in Britain and one of England's biggest telecom companies has purchased units.

HOW: Laurence came up with the idea because his mom was tired of missing mail deliveries and having to go herself to the post office to collect the packages. He then got a little help developing a prototype from one of his parents' friends, herself a successful inventor.

FUN FACT: Smart Bell's speaker emits white noise under the homeowner's voice so it really sounds to someone outside the house that the owner is inside.

RESOURCE: http://www.dailymail.co.uk/sciencetech/article-1394448/Doorbell-tricks-burglars-thinking-youre-home-invented-schoolboy-Laurence-Rook-13.html

30

Newsletter Publisher

You'll make the headlines!

You get articles from people and publish a newsletter on a topic of interest to you. You sell it to subscribers or publish it online.

SUPPLIES

You will need a phone and a computer.

TIME NEEDED

Set aside time to find and contact people who will write articles. Design and production time will depend on the equipment you have, the newsletter's length, and your editing speed. You'll either have to create a website that will be your newsletter, or you'll need to plan to spend time seeking subscribers for your print newsletter.

WHAT TO CHARGE

Give away the newsletter, but charge businesses to advertise in your newsletter. For example, if Joe's Bakery wants to advertise doughnuts, the owner of the bakery will be willing to pay you a fee to have advertising space in your paper. The more copies you sell, the more you can charge for advertising space, because owners want many people to see their advertisements. When you are starting out, charge $10 for a quarter-page advertisement. You can charge the same for a similar-size ad online; leave it up for one issue, just as the ads in a paper newsletter last for one issue.

HOW TO ADVERTISE

The best way to advertise your newsletter is to give it directly to the people who would be interested. For instance, if you are publishing a biking newsletter, give out the newsletter at bike events, parks, and trailheads, and stores to buy copies. Find the best place for your type of newsletter. If you're publishing it online, point people to your website by talking about it in biking forums.

HINTS

* Make your newsletter as attractive as possible. The more attractive the newsletter, the more copies you will move. The more people reading your newsletter, the more business owners will want to advertise with you. And all of that leads to: more money in your wallet!
* Several famous magazines started as newsletters. Yours may be the next.

31

Newspaper Mover

Curb-to-door service!

Newspapers are not as common as they once were, but they are still read by many people. Newspaper delivery people usually throw newspapers in their customers' driveways. People have to put on shoes and a jacket, and in many places boots, to go out and get the paper. To serve customers, you get up early in the morning and move their newspapers from the driveway to the front door. When people use your service, they only have to open the door and pick up the paper!

SUPPLIES

You will need flyers, a notepad on which to keep the names and addresses of your customers, and warm clothes if you live in a cold climate.

TIME NEEDED

The time you spend will depend on the number of customers you have. Moving twenty newspapers takes about thirty minutes. You need to be an early riser to do this business. You must move the newspapers before your customers awake, so get up around 5 AM and hit the road early!

WHAT TO CHARGE

$6 per month. Remind potential customers that this price is really only 20 cents per day!

HOW TO ADVERTISE

Use the door-to-door advertising technique. If a customer likes your idea, collect payment for the first month and tell the customer you will start service the next day.

Design a flyer to place next to newspapers early in the morning. Your flyer might say: "Do you dislike having to get dressed and go out in the cold to get the newspaper? I will move your newspaper to your doorstep early in the morning for a small fee. All you'll have to do is open the door to get your paper. Call Skip D. Walk, a responsible kid, at 123-4567 or email Skip@email.com." Early one morning, go out and place one of the flyers next to each newspaper in the neighborhood.

HINTS

* This is a business that can be expanded easily to other neighborhoods. If you can't handle other neighborhoods yourself, look into hiring other kids.

* From time to time, leave a small note with each customer's newspaper on the doorstep. The note might say: "If you enjoyed not having to go outside to get your newspaper this morning, pass this flyer on to a friend or neighbor who would appreciate this service. Newspaper moving from driveway to door early in the morning by Skip D. Walk, a responsible kid. Call 123-4567 or email Skip@email.com."

* Consider providing a special service for your customers. Tell them you will call for another newspaper if you find their paper in a puddle or otherwise destroyed. When you go out to move papers, write down which ones are damaged. Leave a note on the door that says: "I found your paper this way. I've called for a replacement that the company has promised will arrive by 10 a.m." Return to your house and make calls to the newspaper company for customers whose papers were damaged.

32

Online Advisor

Surf the internet with a business purpose.

You're a kid, a consumer, and a tech whiz. Help local business owners make their businesses more prominent online with social media, directories, and search rankings.

SUPPLIES

You should have a computer and reliable internet access.

TIME NEEDED

This will vary based on your clients' needs and your schedule, but what it probably won't be is done in a day or even a week. You know that making customers, like making friends, takes time. You should talk with your client about how many hours you can work per week and set a contract for a month or longer, at which point you two can renegotiate based on how things have been going.

WHAT TO CHARGE

$7.25 per hour. Download a free computer-based timer to keep a record of the time you spend. You can submit this with your invoice—and it may help you see certain patterns so you know which of your techniques are working for which customers. Knowing that can help you improve your work—and earn more money!

HOW TO ADVERTISE

Online, of course! But you should also contact businesses in person. If they need an online advisor, they may not have the time or the skills to find that help online.

HINTS

* Because you'll be working on the same websites, forums, and social media sites that you talk to your friends on, be careful that you don't mix business and pleasure!
* You can guess pretty accurately when your customer's potential customers will be online. If your client is a coffee shop that's only open till lunch, you know the people interested in it are awake, and probably online, in the mornings. So you should make sure you've posted new content the night before or that you're online chatting about the coffee shop in the morning. There are also days and times that the internet is busiest in general. Learn what those currently are so that you're always posting when someone's paying attention!
* The internet is a casual place, and you should use what you know as a kid to help your client get more customers: making conversation with, telling jokes to, and asking questions of other people online. But always be professional. You're a representative of this other company. And always practice internet safety.
* Learn more about how to measure online marketing and sales success and offer an evaluation service for an extra fee.
* You may want to prepare a report for your clients, if they want to do more online talking with kid customers themselves. Help them understand how to use certain technology and how kids use it. Charge an extra fee for this.

33

Online Seller

*One person's junk is
another person's treasure!*

Run customers' online auctions, stores, or classified ads. People
with lots of stuff to sell but little time or tech knowledge will
flock to you.

SUPPLIES

You'll need a dedicated computer and a reliable internet connection that you can access at any time. You'll be more successful if
you also have a digital camera or a quality camera on your phone
so you can take and post photos of the merchandise.

TIME NEEDED

This will vary based on your clients' needs and your schedule, but
what it probably won't be is done in a day or even a week. If you
only have one item to sell, it could be a short project, but most customers would probably like you to sell several items at once or over
a longer period of time. You should talk with your client about
how many hours you can work per week and set a contract for a
month or longer, at which point you two can renegotiate based on
how things have been going.

WHAT TO CHARGE

Take a commission, 10 percent on each item sold. The buyer pays you once the item has sold.

HOW TO ADVERTISE

Advertise or post in the forums related to the sites you would sell on.

Stop at garage and estate sales toward the end of the sale and talk to the homeowners. You might say something like, "Looks like you had a good sale, but I see there's still a lot of cool stuff left. Why spend another weekend running a garage sale? I'll sell your items online and charge you a lower commission than other sales services do—and I'll make you more money."

If a person is still unsure, remind that person that you're not just sitting in front of the computer screen for them. You'll research the market for each item so the two of you can determine the best ask and sale prices possible, you'll write about the product and take its picture for the ad, and you'll write a catchy title that will grab buyers' eyes. And yes, you'll be sitting in front of the computer—watching the bids roll in!

HINTS

* Some of the sales sites require users to be 18, so you may have to enlist an older sibling or parent to help.
* Leave the items to be sold at your client's home. Arrange to take photos of the items there, and when the item sells, contact your client right away so they can properly package and ship the item. If a buyer wants to look at the item before deciding, work with the client to make an appointment, and your client will do any in-person work with the buyer.
* Learn more about the site you're posting to. What do other people sell there and how do they sell it—phrases they use in their descriptions, if there's a system so you can be rated as a trustworthy seller, etc.

* Make the photos you take useful. If it's important that the buyer understand the size of an item, take a photo of it next to something standard and recognizable, like a quarter, a dollar bill, or a pop can. Don't use photos of a similar item you find online—not only is that misleading to the customer but it could be copyright infringement.

* For online auction sites, think about when likely customers will be online. A lot of people are busy on Friday and Saturday nights but they are home Sunday nights, so you may not want your auction to end on a Friday or Saturday.

* You can expand your business into marketing for some clients. Those with an ongoing business selling items they make, for example, may be interested in you advising them on designing a better website and strengthening their social media use.

* Don't get distracted and shop for yourself! You're on company time, so bookmark the site and return during your free time.

* Even though you'll be taking a commission, and not working for an hourly wage, it's a good idea to keep track of the time you work anyway—for your client's records and for yours.

INSPIRATION FROM KID ENTREPRENEURS JUST LIKE YOU!

NAME: Alex Mangini

TITLE: blogger, web designer, business owner

AGE: 17

WHERE: New Jersey, USA

WHAT: With more than five thousand monthly readers, Alex is one of the highest-ranking teen bloggers. He blogs about blogging—everything from the science and psychology of it to a blog's aesthetics and functionality—and he owns a company that provides resources for a major niche market in website design.

HOW: From his dad, who owns two restaurants, Alex learned two things: one, that he doesn't like to sit still either, and two, he doesn't want to wake up one day stuck in a job he doesn't like. He now knows that working in a restaurant is not for him, so he's studying hard in high school and launching businesses that he does like, now, not later.

FUN FACT: A fun quote from Alex: "I like the idea of working hard now, so you can earn big later."

RESOURCES: www.blogussion.com
http://kolakube.com

34

Party Helper

The perfect host
will need you most!

People who need help at a party hire you. You assist by greeting guests, taking coats, serving food, cleaning up after the party, and doing other chores for the host.

SUPPLIES

You will need a phone, advertising, appropriate clothes, and a positive attitude. Your clothes should be clean and tidy but not too attention-catching. Remember, you're helping at the party, not giving it.

TIME NEEDED

The average party lasts between three and five hours. Parties may last longer than the host expects. Set aside time to stay as long as the host needs you. You will be busiest Friday and Saturday evenings. Some people will want you to help at other times such as Sunday-morning brunches or midweek gatherings.

WHAT TO CHARGE

$7.25 per hour that you work. If the location is outside your neighborhood, you may also charge for travel time and the cost of getting there.

HOW TO ADVERTISE

Distribute flyers to houses in your neighborhood about one week before each major holiday. People give many parties during the holiday seasons. Your flyer might say: "Planning a party for the holiday? I'd like to help by greeting guests, serving food, clearing the table, washing dishes, and doing whatever else you need. Call Par T. Helper at 123-4567 or email Par@email.com."

Another creative approach is to dress as a butler and visit houses before the holiday seasons. When homeowners answer the door, describe your service.

Once you gain a few satisfied customers, collect letters from them saying how much they appreciate your help. Be sure the letters have phone numbers, so potential customers can call your references.

HINTS

* You'll have to dress appropriately for each occasion. When customers call to arrange your visit, ask what type of party they are giving. If the event is a fancy dinner party, you'll need to dress up—nice pants, a button-down shirt, and a tie for boys, a dress or skirt for girls. If the gathering is a cowboy barbecue, you might consider jeans and other Western attire. Whatever you wear, be sure you look neat and orderly. Carry a few of your flyers in your pocket when you work, because guests at the party might be interested in your service.
* Offer to entertain young children during the party. Bring games to play with them and prizes to reward them. Try to keep the children away from other guests, so the adults can enjoy the party.

* Arrive early. Help the customer set up. Offer to vacuum or clean. During the party, be courteous to hosts and guests and quickly get whatever they request. After the party, clean up promptly and don't leave until you have tidied up everything.
* Then collect your money.

35

Phone Information-Line Organizer

You make the call!

You run a phone message system for people to call and receive information. You can leave a joke message, video-game-tip message, or baseball-card-hobby message. Think of your own creative theme. People don't have to pay to call. You make your money by selling advertisements to local store owners to put at the beginning of your message. When people call, first they hear the store's advertisements, then the information.

SUPPLIES

You will need a dedicated phone number—a number that is used only for the business.

TIME NEEDED

You will need to change the message every morning, so the time involved is only ten minutes daily. Plan on spending time each week writing the scripts for the next week's messages. Plan on spending more time to sell advertisements to local business owners.

WHAT TO CHARGE

$10 per week for a twenty-second advertisement. You don't want to overwhelm your message with ads, burying the information in your message, but you can have several advertisements on the line. Therefore, you can earn more than $10 per week.

HOW TO ADVERTISE

There are two types of advertisements in this business. First, you advertise the phone line to small businesses, so they will buy advertising time from you for your phone line. Second, you advertise your phone line to the public so people will call.

To get local business owners to buy advertising time, distribute flyers to small businesses in your area and introduce yourself to owners. You will have to convince them that many people will call your phone line and that those people would also be interested in shopping at that store. Remember, small-business owners will buy advertising time on your line only if many phone callers will hear about the owners' businesses.

To advertise to the public and to get callers, be sure to mention that the phone call is free to local callers.

HINTS

* You can set up a phone line easily. Use your phone or use one of the many free or inexpensive online voicemail services. Record your first day's message. On a joke line, you might say: "Hello, thank you for calling the Daily Joke Phone Line. Today's message is sponsored by Main Street Books, which offers a complete line of hilarious joke books. Mention the Daily Joke Line and receive a 10 percent discount on any book in the store. Main Street Books is located at 232 Main Street. Call 123-4567 for more information. Now, for today's joke . . ." Record a funny joke at the end of the message, but keep the entire recording to less than a minute. Imagine how much fun this line can be!

36

Photograph Organizer

Share the memories!

People like to take photographs but often don't have time to organize them. You arrange customers' pictures and put them in binder or online albums. If the customer wishes, you label and date the photographs. You decorate pages in the album to make them look attractive.

SUPPLIES

You will need a phone, computer, and advertising. Some customers will want a basic online photo album. If so, that's all you need! For those who have boxes of old printed photos that need organizing, bring scissors, labels, a variety of colored pens and pencils, and colored paper. And some people would like you to scrapbook their pictures—there are lots of stores online and off that offer more decorations than you could ever use. Don't invest ahead of projects in albums because they're more expensive—use your customers' albums or consult with them about what they want you to buy.

TIME NEEDED

To put together a full album will take one to twelve hours, depending on how much time you spend decorating each page. Allow time to buy supplies and advertise.

WHAT TO CHARGE

For online albums, charge $7.25 an hour. For other types, a flat project fee is often best, and you can offer tiered packages based on how large or elaborately decorated an album the customer wants. For example, $15 for a basic album, $45 for a scrapbook. Remind customers that your fee includes all supplies except the album itself. If your customers want you to buy albums, add the cost to your price.

HOW TO ADVERTISE

Distribute flyers in your neighborhood about a week after holidays. People go away over holidays and take many pictures. They realize later that they don't have the time to organize the photos or put together an album. They see your flyer and call you.

Your flyer might say: "Are your photographs stacked up in drawers? Is your camera's memory card full? Let a creative and organized kid do the work for you cheaply. I can make anything from an online album to a scrapbook. Call 123-4567 or email photoorganizer@email.com."

HINTS

* When you put the albums together, make them look attractive. Discuss decorating ideas with customers before doing the work. To learn more, watch how-to videos online, check out scrapbooking books from the library, or talk with the staff at scrapbooking or art stores.

* You can promote your business by putting a picture of your own in the albums. Make a big poster that says: "This album was arranged by PhotoOrganizer.com. Call 123-4567." Have someone take a picture of you holding the poster. Put one of your pictures in the back of each album to remind people of your service!

* As an extra service, offer to upload some of the photos from an online album to the customer's social media account or email the link to his new album to his address book; take customers' film to a developer and bring back prints; or make a paper album, at a discounted rate, to complement an online album, or an online album in addition to the paper album that the customer ordered. Charge more for these services.

INSPIRATION FROM KID ENTREPRENEURS JUST LIKE YOU!

NAME: Tavi Gevinson

TITLE: media and fashion pro

AGE: 15

WHERE: Chicago, USA

WHAT: Since 2008, when she was twelve years old, Tavi has been blogging about fashion, design, and generally being a culturally curious and aware girl growing up. She and Jane Pratt, founder of *Sassy* magazine, are collaborating on a new magazine; she's shopping a nonfiction book to publishers; and she's working on a coffee-table book based on her blog.

HOW: Capitalizing on her strong writing voice and work ethic, Tavi has developed a huge online following and scores front-row seats at big-city fashion weeks.

FUN FACT: Tavi is not on Facebook, and she idolizes the cartoon character Daria, whose MTV show ended before Tavi had lost all of her baby teeth.

RESOURCE: www.thestylerookie.com

37

Photographer

*A picture is worth
more than a thousand words!*

You take photographs or videos at parties, weddings, and other important events. By charging much less than professionals and doing excellent work, you will build a successful business.

SUPPLIES

You will need a phone, advertising, appropriate clothes, and a digital camera or video camera.

TIME NEEDED

The average party lasts four hours. You will need to meet with customers for about an hour several weeks before the party to clarify exactly what they want. You will want to arrive a half hour before the party to set up equipment, check the lighting, and meet with the host.

WHAT TO CHARGE

$15 per hour.

HOW TO ADVERTISE

Ask at local party-supply stores if you can leave flyers on their counters. Tell owners you will refer business to them if they allow you to leave the flyers.

Visit professional party djs in your area and introduce yourself. Ask them to recommend you to customers having parties in the near future.

Before the holiday season, distribute flyers in your neighborhood. The flyer might say: "Planning a party? Hate missing the fun while you take pictures or video? Want to avoid the high cost of professional photography? Call Cam E. Rah, a kid who is a talented amateur photographer, at 123-4567 for inexpensive party pictures and videos."

For casual parties, advertise while you work. Use shirt paints to make a shirt that says: "Party pictures and videos by Cam E. Rah. Call 123-4567." Wear the shirt to advertise your business while you work.

HINTS

* Create a portfolio showing the best examples of your work, accessible both online and as a book that you can show at meetings. Also collect quotes from satisfied customers.
* At parties, dress appropriately and be polite to partygoers. Try to take at least one picture of every guest. Carry several of your flyers or business cards, so you can give them to people who ask about your service.
* Upload the photos or video to the web, or if you give them to the customer on a CD or flash drive, make sure you label the files professionally and appropriately so the customer knows what each picture is without even opening it.

38

Price Shopper

*Search high and low
for the best deal.*

Most people want to find the cheapest prices before they make large purchases. They often don't have the time or know-how to locate the best deals. Customers send you a short description of a product they would like to buy. You research prices online and maybe by calling area stores. You report back to customers and inform them of the website or store that has the cheapest price for the product they requested.

SUPPLIES

You will need a phone, a computer, and a reliable internet connection.

TIME NEEDED

You will spend five to fifteen minutes speaking with customers to find out exactly what they need. Set aside one to two hours to research the product and find the cheapest price. Research time may be longer, depending on the type of product.

WHAT TO CHARGE

$10 per product the customer requests. Have customers pay after you complete the search.

HOW TO ADVERTISE

Distribute flyers in your neighborhood. You might say: "Want to save money but don't have time to find the cheapest prices on products? Let me do the search for you. I will save you time and money. Send a short description of the product you want to Lois Price, Lois@email.com. Once I find you the cheapest price, I will bill you for $10. I am an efficient kid who will work hard to save you money. Call 123-4567 for more information."

HINTS

* You can offer another service related to this business. Customers call and ask you for consumer information on products they are considering for purchase. You learn as much as you can about the products by visiting stores, making calls, and reading customer and professional reviews online. You present the information to your customers so that they can choose the type of product they want. For instance, computers come in many different speeds and powers and with different kinds of monitors. Someone who knows nothing about computers but wants to buy one calls you. You learn about different specifications and present your knowledge to the customer. You charge between $20 and $30 for this service.
* You will be busiest around holiday time, because people will be buying products as gifts. Be sure to be home before the holiday season.

39

Puppet Maker

Bring characters to life.

You make unique puppets from a variety of materials. You sell your merchandise to neighbors and people at fairs. Stores may buy your puppets and sell them to the public.

SUPPLIES

You will need a phone or a computer to take orders. You can buy materials to make puppets at craft stores and fabric centers. Don't overlook online sites, garage sales, and recycling centers where you might find inexpensive or even free interesting materials to make your puppets. A sewing machine is helpful but not necessary.

TIME NEEDED

Making a detailed puppet takes about two hours. If your puppets become popular, you will have to make them a little faster in order to turn out enough.

WHAT TO CHARGE

If you sell directly to the public online, at fairs, or door-to-door, charge $15 per puppet plus packaging and shipping or delivery. If you sell to stores, expect to have to charge less, but you might be able to make that up by selling each store more than one puppet.

HOW TO ADVERTISE

If you sell at a fair, have your puppets sell themselves by making them "talk" to people who walk by your stand. For instance, make your puppets say to adults, "Your child would love to play with me. For a little money, you can take me home." To children, make your puppets say, "Hi! I'm lots of fun to play with. Ask your parents to buy me." You don't have to be a ventriloquist. Just try your best to be persuasive and entertaining. When going door-to-door to sell puppets, put one on each hand and have them make the presentation for you. As an introductory offer, say you'll give one puppet free if the person buys three.

If you're selling to small businesses such as toy stores and gift shops, introduce yourself to business owners and present samples of your puppets. Offer to sell your merchandise on consignment, which means that store owners pay you only if the puppets sell.

Try to sell your line of puppets to a big department store. Write a letter describing your product. Take pictures of your puppets and enclose them in the letter. Send it to the buyer of children's toys at a department store. You can ask a librarian to show you a book that contains the addresses of buyers. You may not receive many responses, but if just one department store likes your idea, you can sell hundreds of puppets!

HINTS

* The best time to promote your merchandise is before holidays. At this time of year, go door-to-door in your neighborhood.
* Several websites, online videos, and books exist on designing and making puppets. Go online or to your local library and check them out for ideas before you begin this business.

INSPIRATION FROM KID ENTREPRENEURS JUST LIKE YOU!

NAME: Tyler Page

TITLE: philanthropist, nonprofit founder

AGE: 14

WHERE: California, USA

WHAT: Tyler is the founder of Kids Helping Kids Leadership Academy, Inc., a nonprofit organization that both raises funds to help kids and teaches kids how to raise funds for others in need.

HOW: When he was ten years old, Tyler Page saw an *Oprah* show that talked about children sold into slavery in western Africa. Moved by this, Tyler organized a car wash to help some of these children avoid this fate. After the car wash, he figured he raised enough money to save four kids—and he immediately wondered, what about that fifth kid? He could keep raising money on his own, as he has, but he also realized that a lot of other kids wanted to help, too! With his mom's help, he created Kids Helping Kids to support other young philanthropists with curriculums, meetings, projects, and more resources.

FUN FACT: Tyler's organization invites kids around the world to join his "lemonade stand challenge" every June–August—and just as this book does, the challenge encourages kids to do whatever work is most exciting to them, whether that's running a lemonade stand or beyond.

RESOURCE: www.kidzhelpingkids.org

40

Recycler

Reduce, reuse, recycle!

Not all cities and towns offer regular curbside recycling, and most services don't recycle everything at the curb. You ask neighbors, businesses, and schools to save the recyclables their disposal service won't collect. Weekly, on the day you arrange, they put the bagged or boxed items outside their home for you to pick up. You take them to a nearby recycling center.

SUPPLIES

You will need a cart or wagon, a storage area for the materials, an adult with a car to help you take the materials to the recycling center, and flyers. A garage or backyard shed works best as a storage area.

TIME NEEDED

You decide which day to pick up the newspapers and cans. For every fifteen locations from which you pick up, count on spending one hour. Remember, your cart can hold only a limited quantity of newspapers and cans. You'll have to return to your storage area to empty the cart.

WHAT TO CHARGE

$2.50 per visit. Try to get customers to pay you for a month in advance.

HOW TO ADVERTISE

Distribute flyers to businesses, schools, other organizations in your area, and homes. In the flyers, you might draw a picture of Earth and write: "Put your extra recycling or the items your garbage service won't pick up, on the curb every Friday night to be collected for recycling. An earth-loving kid will transport the materials to a recycling center for only $2.50. If you have questions, call Rhea Cycle at 123-4567."

HINTS

* Friday night is often the best time for people to put the materials out, because you can collect them Saturday morning.
* Most businesses have an all-encompassing disposal service, but some do not. Talk with local store owners about recycling what they don't.

41

Rock Painter

Leave no stone unturned.

You decorate rocks so they resemble people, animals, and other figures. To decorate the rocks, you use paint, glitter, fabric, and anything else you can find. You sell them directly to the public at fairs and craft shows. Stores may wish to buy your rocks and resell them.

SUPPLIES

You will need a phone or computer, flyers, rocks, and the rock-decorating materials. You'll need a decent supply of artistic talent to run this business! Go to an art supply store or a craft store to find the decorations. Shirt paints and colored glue are the best to use on rocks. Ask at your local hardware store about other paints that are suitable for painting rocks. The rocks shouldn't be hard to find!

TIME NEEDED

Decorating rocks will take only about fifteen minutes per rock, but selling them will take more time. If you sell them at fairs, plan to spend the day. If you sell them to stores, time will be needed to visit owners and present your merchandise. If you sell online, you can do so all day any day you're not at school or for just a few minutes between homework and bed.

WHAT TO CHARGE

If you sell your rocks at fairs, charge between $1 and $5, depending on size and decoration. When dealing with stores, you should be prepared to charge less—but maybe you can make some of that difference up by selling in bulk.

HOW TO ADVERTISE

To sell your rocks at fairs, put up a large sign, which might say: "Rock Figurines Made by Mark D. Stone." Cover your table at the fair with your decorated rocks and display them nicely. You can lay the rocks out on tissue paper or put them on little pedestals. To sell your rocks to stores, use the door-to-door advertising method. Try to sell to gift shops first. They are most likely to be interested in your product. Introduce yourself to owners and show samples of your work. You can give each business owner a sample rock and flyer. On the back of the samples, write your name and phone number in big letters.

HINTS

* Make your rocks unique. Create animal rocks, appliance rocks, and rocks that look like celebrities.
* Consider cute phrases to put on your rocks. For instance, paint a musical note and write the words "Rock Concert" on the rock. Paint a picture of a road and write the words "Rocky Road." Consider longer lines too. Draw a picture of a cradle and write "Don't rock the cradle." Paint a hammer and write "Solid as a rock." Think of other phrases.
* Using a thin-tip felt marker, write your name on the bottom of every rock you decorate. People will recognize your rocks when they see them.

42

Seedling Grower

Flower power!

You act as a plant nursery, nurturing the plants from seeds to seedlings. Everyone likes having a healthy garden or beautiful plants in their homes, and buying plants as seeds is the cheapest way to do so. But getting the seeds to survive long enough to become healthy "toddler" plants requires patience and attention to detail, and many people don't have the time or interest that is needed. They will be your customers.

SUPPLIES

You will need containers, potting mix, seeds, labels and permanent markers, plastic bags or other plastic covers that will fit your containers, water, light, and advertising.

TIME NEEDED

Plan on needing time to choose and buy seeds, online or at a store, and prepare the potting mix. Once you've planted the seeds, you will need to check in on them every day and tend to their needs. This will only take a few seconds to minutes a day.

WHAT TO CHARGE

$1 to $5 per plant depending on the size and type of plant.

HOW TO ADVERTISE

Ask plant stores and nurseries if you can leave flyers near their registers, and if they would directly recommend your service to anyone who buys seeds. Tell them you'll refer people to their store in return.

Approach neighbors when you see them working outside in their gardens and yards. You might say something like, "Those are beautiful sunflowers! Wouldn't some thyme make a nice border around them? For next year, I'll start the plant from seed, keep it healthy and growing in the late winter and spring, and then deliver it to you ready for you to plant it in your garden."

When you give the seedling to your neighbor, give them a sheet of tips on caring for their plant and include your name and contact information on the sheet.

Make a beautiful or fun plant tag for your customer's garden. With a cleaned popsicle stick, paper, and waterproof markers, you can make a tag that says something like: "This poppy was born in March at G. R. Owing's house. Call 123-4567 or email GR@ email.com if you'd like a healthy plant like this in your garden!"

HINTS

* Don't ever buy new plastic pots! You can use egg cartons or yogurt tubs. Also, gardeners are always getting rid of them. Put a sign up at your local grocery stores and nurseries, offering to take pots off their hands for free. Then wash them carefully to make sure they are disease free before using them.
* Helping plants survive infancy takes finesse, but planting them is physically easy:
* Loosen and dampen the potting mix and fill each container about two-thirds full; don't press the mix down. Follow the

directions on your seed packets, but usually you can just sprinkle them from the bag into the pot and then gently cover them with more dampened mix. Use at least three seeds per container because not all will survive.

* Water some more. Label each container, so you don't forget which plant is which, and to which customer it's going!

* Loosely cover the containers with a plastic baggie or with plastic wrap to trap heat and moisture—you're creating a tiny greenhouse. Set the plants in a warm place that's not drafty.

* Keep the dirt wet but not drowning.

* Move the plant into indirect sun and remove its cover as soon as you see a seedling. Once the seedling has started to uncurl, move the plant into direct light—under indoor light or winter sun, your seedling may need up to eighteen hours of light each day.

* The first two "leaves" you'll see won't be true leaves; wait till your plant gets a little bigger and then add some fertilizer to the pot. If more than one seedling grows and you want to separate them, don't just yank them from the pot—you could easily damage their roots, which have likely tangled together.

* If your customers already have seeds, charge them less. Many will want you to buy the seeds still, but they will want to pick what types of plants. A few customers will want you to do everything, including choosing the plants! Before you buy the seeds, talk with them about what they like and don't like and where the plant will live, so you know if you should buy seeds for plants that do well in pots or in the ground, in sun or in shade.

* Learn about plants that grow well in your area at each time of year. Research online or at the library, or ask for help at your local plant store. Most people who work at nurseries love to help people learn how to treat plants well. If you can suggest plants with knowledge and confidence, your clients will have confidence in you and you'll get repeat business.

* You can harvest seeds from your own garden or buy them online or at a store. Don't buy too many in advance, because you don't want to use old seeds that might not grow as well as fresher ones.

* You will have greater success if you use dirt made specifically for potted plants. Outdoor soil compacts too much and can carry weed seeds and disease spores. Look for bags labeled as soilless or for indoor plants. Or learn online how to make your own!

* You want to sign up most of your clients at the seed stage, but you can sell once the seeds have become seedlings, too. You can sell them in their planting containers, at fairs or at a sidewalk stand you set up, or you can transfer them into prettier (but still affordable!) containers and sell them that way. If you're growing flowers or vegetables, you may be able to keep the plants for yourself and sell some of your harvest!

43

(citrus slice illustration)

Senior Helper

Experience the wisdom of age.

You assist seniors by running errands, cooking, watering plants, reading to them, or doing other useful tasks. You not only earn money but you contribute to the community by helping older people.

SUPPLIES

You will need advertising and a phone.

TIME NEEDED

The time depends on the services each customer requests. Certain customers may want you to cook and clean every night, and others may ask you to come and read to them once a week. You will need to be available at different times of the day, because customers will need you at odd hours.

WHAT TO CHARGE

Ask $5 per hour. Some of your older customers may not be able to afford a higher amount.

HOW TO ADVERTISE

Distribute flyers in your area. Describe your service clearly. Here's an example: "I am a kid who would like to help seniors. I can cook, clean, water plants, and do other chores. I can read to you and provide you with company. Call Erin Doer at 123-4567." You may be able to offer an email contact option, but a lot of older people prefer the phone.

You may want to do door-to-door advertising. Knock on the door, introduce yourself, explain your service, and ask if elderly people live in the house. If there are none, ask if they know of an older neighbor who might need your services. If the person at the door is a senior or says that an older person is living in the house, explain your service further and be sure to leave one of your flyers.

Locate religious organizations, retirement homes, and other clubs and places that seniors frequent. Ask to place a small advertisement describing your service in their newsletters and bulletins.

HINTS

* Be sure to make regular checkup calls. Phone your customers frequently to see how they are doing. They might need something and would appreciate a phone call.
* During holiday seasons, you can bring fresh flowers to brighten your customers' homes. Cook dinners for your customers on the eves of special holidays. During other times of the year, you can bake cookies or brownies to share a special no-reason treat.
* Older seniors are sometimes hesitant to take walks alone. You can accompany them on walks to the park or through the neighborhood.
* Enjoy your visits with seniors. Talking with older people can be extremely interesting, because they have lived through events you have only read about in history books. When you do reports for history class, you can get ideas and firsthand accounts from your clients. Ask them to tell you their life stories. You'll be amazed at what you hear.

44

Sheet and Towel Washer

Do you have the knack to wash, dry, fold, and stack?

You visit customers' houses once a week and wash and change the sheets and towels. You put clean sheets on the beds and put out fresh towels in the bathrooms and kitchen. People in your neighborhood who don't have the time or energy to do this chore will appreciate your service.

SUPPLIES

You don't need much to start this business except a willingness to handle dirty laundry!

TIME NEEDED

Washing and changing the sheets and towels in most houses will take about two hours. You will spend most of the time waiting for the washing machine and dryer to complete their cycles. You can bring your homework and study, a book or magazine and read, or music with headphones and just relax while the washing machine works! If you have several customers nearby, you can save time by working in other houses while waiting for the machines to finish their cycles.

WHAT TO CHARGE

Collect your fee of $50 per month at the beginning of each month.
Charge more if your customers want you to do other house chores,
such as taking out the garbage, washing dishes, or cleaning up the
kids' rooms.

HOW TO ADVERTISE

Knock on doors in your neighborhood, introduce yourself, and
describe your service. If customers are unsure, offer to do the
sheets and towels for free the first time, so they can see the quality
of your work. If people still reject your service, give them one of
your flyers so they can call you in the future. Many supermarkets
have free advertising boards where you can place index cards. You

might write: "Tired of doing dirty sheets and towels? Fed up with spending your time in the laundry room? Have your sheets and towels expertly washed and changed in your home by an honest kid for a small fee. Call Lynn N. Washer at 123-4567 or email Lynn@email.com."

HINTS

* On your first visit to a house, ask the customer to teach you how to use their washing machine and dryer. Ask them what temperature they want you to use when washing and drying their linens. Request that they show you which sheets and towels are to be washed and changed. People usually want their beds made and towels folded in a certain way, so be sure you know what they want before you start.

* Make a schedule, and don't plan to do too many houses on a single day. Always be on time. If you are scheduled to be at a customer's house every Thursday at 5 PM, be there at 5 PM, not 5:01 and definitely not 5:15. Customers will appreciate your timeliness.

* Some customers may want you to iron linens. If you do, be careful not to burn the sheets or yourself. Because ironing requires extra time, charge more for this service.

INSPIRATION FROM KID ENTREPRENEURS JUST LIKE YOU!

NAME: Wyatt Workman

TITLE: artist, filmmaker, environmentalist

AGE: 8

WHERE: California, USA

WHAT: *Save the Sea from the Trash Monster* is Wyatt's first claymation movie. He's since published a book based on the movie, has designed "I am NOT a Trash Monster!" bumper stickers, buttons, and T-shirts, and continues to make clay artwork based on the movie's creatures, all of which he sells online, at special events, and art shows. He donates his profits to Oceana (www.oceana.org).

HOW: This is our favorite "how" anecdote: Wyatt was inspired by another kid entrepreneur! Wyatt saw another kid artist's paintings online and in addition to thinking they were really cool, he was impressed that this kid was doing his own art show already. But Wyatt didn't want to make a lot of money for himself. He loves the ocean, and hates all the garbage in it, so he decided to start a business to raise funds to improve and protect the ocean.

FUN FACT: From Wyatt's online bio: "Every time I make things with clay, my kittens jump up on the table and put holes in the clay, and that is very helpful." I bet that is very helpful.

RESOURCE: www.wyattsworks.com

45

Shirt Designer

Make a fashion statement!

You paint designs on shirts and sell the shirts at art fairs, carnivals, and door-to-door. Small clothing stores in your area might purchase your merchandise.

SUPPLIES

You will need shirts and paints. Buy many colors of shirt paints when they go on sale at craft stores or online. Purchase shirts from discount stores or online. The success of this business depends on the amount you spend on supplies. Make sure you buy your materials cheaply, but do pay attention to quality.

TIME NEEDED

Decide how much you want to work. Designing each shirt at home will take about a half hour. You can sell your merchandise at an art fair for an entire day or door-to-door for a few hours.

WHAT TO CHARGE

Charge double your cost for the supplies for each shirt. For instance, if you buy a plain shirt for $5 and paints for $1, sell the decorated shirt for $12.

HOW TO ADVERTISE

At art fairs, put up posters that advertise your business. Hang samples of shirts around your stand and wear one, too.

To advertise door-to-door, visit houses in your area before holidays when people give gifts. Show samples of your work to homeowners and ask them to buy a shirt for each of their children or other family members. As an introductory offer, give one shirt free if the customer buys two.

You may want to try to sell to employees of local businesses. Ask permission and then walk through offices in your area and sell your shirts to secretaries, managers, and other workers.

To sell to small clothing stores in your area, carry several samples and visit store owners. If an owner is unsure, give two shirts free and ask the owner to try to sell them. If the shirts sell quickly, the owner will call you and order more. Sell your shirts in groups of five to stores. Charge less than your normal price, because stores need to make a profit, too!

HINTS

* You need to be an excellent shirt painter if you're to succeed in this business. If you've never painted shirts before, research how online—there are websites on design and color and there are how-to videos—or check out books from the library on clothing design and color schemes. Visit art fairs and stores to see how other shirts are painted. Use other designs as ideas, but don't copy them.

* Make different kinds of shirts for each age group. For toddlers, design shirts with rainbows, letters, numbers, and toys. For older kids, paint shirts with pictures of footballs, cars, horses, and flowers. For adults, create shirts with attractive abstract designs. Abstract designs don't necessary resemble an object. They consist of lines, circles, boxes, zigzags, and other shapes.

46

Sign Maker

Turn a mention into big attention!

You design and produce large posters and signs for small businesses in your area. They will order your signs to advertise sales, specials, and other events.

SUPPLIES

You will need stencil sets. Buy five different kinds of letters between six and ten inches tall. Purchase poster paints, markers, poster board, and other decoration materials. Watch for sales at local arts and crafts stores. Go to graphic design studios and ask for old supplies.

TIME NEEDED

Each poster will take about an hour to make. Depending on how far away the customer's business is located, count on between fifteen and thirty minutes to set up the order and another half hour to deliver the poster and collect your money.

WHAT TO CHARGE

$15 per poster. Remind the customer that this price includes the cost of supplies.

HOW TO ADVERTISE

Use the door-to-door technique of advertising. Make a presentable poster to use as a sample. Bring your sample and a pile of flyers and visit small businesses in your area. When you meet a business owner, introduce yourself and explain your service. Show the owner your sample and explain that you can make signs with any words the owner wishes. Offer to make the first sign for $10 instead of $15 as an introductory offer. If the owner is still hesitant, offer to design a free small poster.

Visit stores that already use posters in their windows. Offer to make a better sign for less than they paid. Go to stores that have no window posters and try to convince the owners that posters will greatly improve their business.

HINTS

* When a customer calls you and orders a sign, go to the owner's business. Spend time discussing what the owner wants the sign to say. Draw a sketch of the sign and be sure the customer agrees to the style, layout, and colors. Set a delivery date of two or three days later. Collect half the money on the first visit so you can pay for supplies. Go to a local art store, or any store that sells the supplies you need, and buy them. Make the poster at home. Return to the owner's business to deliver the sign and collect the rest of your money.

* To make money in this business, you will need to conserve your supplies. Try to use your materials wisely and save leftover scraps for future posters. When you buy new materials, look for sales and discounts.

* When you finish making the sign, write your name and contact information in small letters in the bottom right corner. If other small-business owners see the sign and like it, you may have new customers!

47

Silver Polisher

Serve it up on a silver platter!

You make tarnished, gray silver beautiful and shiny! You go to customers' houses and polish silver dishes, cups, utensils, jewelry, and other small silver household items. You wash them to remove the polish and dry them to make them shine.

SUPPLIES

You will need a phone or computer, flyers, dishcloths, toothpaste and baking soda, and rubber gloves. Use clean old shirts and cloth baby diapers as dishcloths.

TIME NEEDED

Each silver piece will take about three minutes to polish. Washing and drying will take another two minutes. Making your own polish takes almost no time, or money, at all—you can use straight toothpaste, or mix baking soda and water into a paste.

WHAT TO CHARGE

$7.25 per hour. Remind the customer that for this price, you supply the silver polish and dishcloths. Certain customers will want to pay you for each piece you clean. In this case, charge $1 per dish or cup and 50 cents per utensil. Request more for large bowls, trays, and other serving containers.

HOW TO ADVERTISE

Distribute flyers in your area four weeks before holidays. People usually want clean silver to use at holiday dinners and parties. Your flyer might say: "Is your silver dull and tarnished? Does it look like it has been in an attic for years? No time or energy to clean it? Let a tireless kid polish and restore your silver until it shines! Call Paul Isher at 123-4567 or email Paul@email.com for reasonable rates." When a customer contacts you, arrange a time to visit.

Go door-to-door carrying two pieces of your parents' silver. One should be dirty and tarnished and the other clean and shiny. You might say: "Hi, I'm Paul Isher. Does your silver look old and grimy like this or new and shiny like this? I'll polish, wash, and dry your silver for only $7.25 per hour. This price includes rags and polish. All you have to supply is the silver and the sink."

Seniors use silver table settings more than younger families do, so approach your older neighbors first.

HINTS

* Try not to make a mess in your customers' houses. Be sure to wear an old shirt, in case you make a mess of yourself!
* But remember that you're working with toothpaste and baking soda only. Advertise your service as green, because it is!
* Silver polishing is quite easy. Wipe each piece with toothpaste or baking-soda paste. Be sure to wipe every crevice of the silver pieces. When you finish polishing, wash the silver thoroughly with soap and water to remove the polish. Dry the silver pieces

and put them out on the counter so the customer can see the work you've done. Collect your money and leave five flyers for the customer to pass on to friends.

* Silver becomes tarnished quickly, so you could have repeat customers, but people don't use silver much anymore. Keep a notebook of customers and call them after several months to see if their silver needs polishing again, but you may find your heaviest business is always right before the holidays.

* You could also approach event spaces, restaurants, and jewelry stores about polishing their stock. They might be interested in your smart environmental methods, or they may have their own system they want you to use.

INSPIRATION FROM KID ENTREPRENEURS JUST LIKE YOU!

NAME: Anna Azevedo

TITLE: business owner, environmentalist

AGE: 10

WHERE: California, USA

WHAT: For her business, Sprout, Anna makes her own plant fertilizer, starts plants in her backyard garden, and then pots the plants in used drinking glasses, recycling the glass in an earth-friendly way.

HOW: Three stars aligned for Anna's starting of her own business: One, she decided she wanted to take horseback riding lessons, but she wanted to earn the cost of the lessons herself. Two, her older brother makes duct-tape wallets and sells them at a local craft fair. And three, Anna attended a sale where houseplants in little glass containers were being sold. She already knew how important plants are to our ecosystem's health, and she thought she could start a money-earning business around that. Her parents gave her a business loan for start-up costs and Anna set a budget and does her own accounting.

FUN FACTS: Sprout's first plants came from clippings Anna took from her own family's ivy, kangaroo ferns, grass, and peace lily. Her grandmother is her expert garage-sale hunter.

RESOURCE: annasprout.com

162

48

Snack Vendor

*Sell tasty treats
to hungry people.*

You sell snacks in busy areas to people who are hungry and thirsty. In summer, you sell cold snacks and drinks such as orange juice, pop, popsicles, and frozen fruit and candy bars. In winter, you offer hot chocolate and coffee.

SUPPLIES

You will need a fold-up card table, a cooler, and poster board and markers to make a sign for your stand. Other supplies depend on what you're selling and how you're selling it. You will need an inexpensive orange juicer, a knife, ice, and cups if you plan to sell orange juice. If you decide to sell hot chocolate, you will need cocoa and several insulated jugs to keep the drink warm.

TIME NEEDED

You sell when you want to sell. This business works well on weekends. In summer, you may be able find a busy place to sell your snacks during the week. You can work the entire day or a few hours, whatever you choose. Remember, though, the longer you work, the more money you make!

WHAT TO CHARGE

Be sure to sell your snacks for more than you paid for them. For example, if you buy a candy bar for $1, sell it for $1.50. You can purchase foods like popsicles in large quantity for about 25 cents each, and you can sell them for about four times the cost at $1! Try to keep your selling prices between 50 cents and $2.

HOW TO ADVERTISE

Attach to your card table three big, bright posters that advertise your snacks. Put one poster on each side of the table except the one where you stand. On the posters, write the names of your products in big letters and describe them in an appetizing way. For instance, you might write: "Fresh, cold orange juice," "Steaming hot chocolate," "Rich chocolate candy bars," or "Icy popsicles." This method of advertising attracts customers.

Wave your products to people walking by your stand. Shout out your product descriptions boldly. You can say: "Sir, wouldn't you love an icy popsicle on this hot summer day? It'll refresh you and cool you off."

HINTS

* Don't offer more than three different foods at once, because you want to specialize in the products you sell and not be a full-service restaurant. You will be most successful if you stick to one item.
* Find busy areas to sell your snacks, such as construction sites, parking lots, and parks. This business is unique, because you go to your customers rather than having them come to you.

49

Snow Shoveler

Clear the way!

You shovel snow from customers' walkways and driveways early in the morning before they leave for work. You also work on weekends or whenever customers want your service.

SUPPLIES

You will need a warm jacket and a strong snow shovel. If your parents have a snowblower, ask them to teach you how to use it. It will help you work more quickly, but be careful while using it! To avoid blisters and frostbite, you'll need warm boots and thick, insulated gloves when you shovel.

TIME NEEDED

An average walkway and driveway will take about thirty minutes to clear. You need to be an early riser. If you have five clients, you may have to get up at three in the morning! You must be up early every day to check whether or not heavy snow has fallen during the night. If so, you have to get up and work! If the ground is clear, you can go back to sleep. In this business, be sure to go to sleep early.

WHAT TO CHARGE

$5 per visit. Collect your fee the evening of the day you work.

HOW TO ADVERTISE

Door-to-door advertising is best in this business, because you can present yourself. It is important to persuade customers you will be responsible and shovel early in the morning whenever it snows. If they are hesitant, offer to do the first day free. Remind customers how much they dislike shoveling snow before going to work. You can handle only about five houses before school each morning, so don't over-advertise. If you were to put out flyers, too many people might respond!

HINTS

* If other people in the neighborhood want your service, find another reliable kid who you can pay to work with you in the mornings. If two people work, you can make more money!

You can operate a large business if you have several kids working with you. You arrange to meet the customers and set up the accounts. Assign the kids the five houses closest to them. You will still collect the fees at the end of the day. When you do, make sure customers are pleased with the service. You pay a portion of your profits to the other kids. If you run a large business, charge $6 per visit, pay the kids $3, and keep $3 for yourself.

* Wear warm clothing and boots when you work. You don't want to have to return home because you're too cold. In cold climates, temperatures can plunge below zero and chill you quickly!

* It doesn't always snow overnight—sometimes the snow falls hardest in the middle of the day! Talk with your customers about their interest in your shoveling their driveways after school but before they return home from work.

* If your parents have a snowblower and you can convince them to let you use it, you can do driveways faster. You may be able to do more than five houses. Again, be careful!

INSPIRATION FROM KID ENTREPRENEURS JUST LIKE YOU!

NAME: Winter Vinecki

TITLE: philanthropist, activist

AGE: 12

WHERE: Oregon, USA

WHAT: Winter founded Team Winter, a nonprofit organization that is working to end prostate cancer.

HOW: You could say that Winter was born to be an entrepreneur—as a two-time IronKids National Triathlon champion (a triathlon is a competition with swimming, biking, and running in one race), she has the dedication and perseverance that all successful entrepreneurs have. But she probably didn't expect to become an entrepreneur so early in life—or for the reason she did. When Winter was nine, her father was diagnosed with prostate cancer, and Winter knew she needed to compete not only for fun but to raise awareness and funds for prostate cancer research. Unfortunately, her dad passed away only ten months after his diagnosis and never saw Team Winter emerge from it infancy. But Winter has helped raise more than $300,000 for prostate cancer awareness and research, and athletes around the world race for Team Winter. In 2012 Winter started a world marathon tour, running a marathon on every continent to raise global awareness for prostate cancer, all in honor of her dad.

FUN FACT: The publisher of this book is based in Oregon, so there is some home-state pride for Team Winter, and for students at the University of Oregon who created a documentary about Team Winter.

RESOURCE: www.teamwinter.org

50

Store Window Painter

It's a window
of opportunity!

You paint messages on store windows. Owners hire you to paint sale advertisements, holiday greetings, and special notices. You paint messages inside the window so they can be seen from the outside. Therefore, you paint everything backward!

SUPPLIES

You will need a phone, flyers, and paint supplies. Ask at your local hardware store for paints that can be used on windows and later washed off with soap and water. Before you begin painting windows, test the paint to be sure it washes off. No matter how striking your design is, the business owner won't want it on the windows forever! Above all, you need to have artistic ability to run this business.

TIME NEEDED

Painting each window will take between one and eight hours, depending on the size of the painting requested. Advertising your business will take time, too.

WHAT TO CHARGE

Depending on the size of the window, charge between $10 and
$50 per window. Collect half the money before you start painting,
because you'll have to buy supplies.

HOW TO ADVERTISE

Meet with small-business owners in your area. Give each owner a
flyer and describe your service. You can offer to do a small painting for free to show the owner the quality of your work.

Buy several small panes of glass at a local hardware store. Paint
a colorful picture on one pane and use it as a sample of your art
work. On another, paint samples of messages, such as "Sale" or
"Happy Holidays." On another pane, paint samples of different
lettering styles, or fonts, from which the owner can choose.

HINTS

* Before you begin, sketch in color what you plan to paint and show it to the store owner. Make several sketches until the owner approves of your work. Be sure the owner agrees to your final design. To avoid disagreements, paint on the window exactly what you have sketched on paper.

* Include your name and contact information in small letters in the bottom right corner of the window, so customers can read them from the outside. Other business owners passing by who like the paintings will call you.

* When you are painting a window, be sure to have flyers in your pocket. People seeing you paint will want to know about your service.

* Many business owners like to have their windows decorated all year with different messages. Visit your customers once a month to ask if they need more window paintings. If you please your customers, they will bring you business for years to come.

51

Street Flower Vendor

Sell enough flowers on the road, and your road to success will be lined with flowers!

You sell flowers afternoons and evenings to commuters on their way home. You set up a stand near a busy road where cars can pull over safely.

SUPPLIES

You will need a neon orange jacket so drivers can see you, a money belt for giving change quickly, and two freestanding signs. Buy an ample supply of fresh flowers and wrapping materials. Florists usually use colored cellophane or decorative paper to wrap flowers.

TIME NEEDED

The best time to sell flowers to commuters is between 4:15 and 6:45 in the evening. It will take time to buy the flowers, set up and close down your stand, and purchase supplies. You can work any day you wish, but be sure to sell Friday evenings. Fridays are often best, because people like to buy flowers for the weekend.

WHAT TO CHARGE

Charge $5 more than the price you pay for each bunch of flowers. Increase your prices on the eves of special holidays, when people are more likely to purchase flowers.

HOW TO ADVERTISE

Stand on the sidewalk near a place where drivers can pull over safely or where train commuters will be walking. Put up large signs a half block away on each side of your stand that say: "Fresh flowers, 1/2 block ahead." Make your signs big and bright, so drivers have no problem seeing them if they're driving fast. Wave your flowers to drivers and walkers passing by.

HINTS

* Find a florist who will sell you inexpensive flowers. Check for a wholesale flower market in your area.
* Grow a garden, and you'll really save money! Consider converting your parents' unused backyard into a flower garden. Grow several different kinds of flowers. Go to a nursery and find out as much as you can about the flowers that grow in your area. Schedule your planting so you can pick flowers throughout most of the year.
* Try to have a variety of colors, because the display will be more eye-catching to drivers. Arrange your flowers in attractive bouquets, with six to ten flowers per bunch. Fill your bouquets with greenery, so they look full. Wrap them carefully in cellophane and attach ribbons for extra appeal.
* Be careful! When you are working near traffic, always wear bright clothes and avoid the road. Do not approach cars until they have come to a complete stop.
* Selling on the side of the road or in a train station may be illegal in certain places. If anyone official tells you to leave, pack up quickly and move your stand to another area. You may also be able to contact an official before you even start, to ask the rules.

52

Tech Teacher

*If you're a gadget whiz,
this is your biz!*

In the age of high technology, many people wish to use computers, smart phones, and e-readers but don't know how, or want to know how to use them better. You teach your customers how to use the electronics they have recently purchased. As an additional service, you instruct customers in the use of software and applications. If you're good enough, companies and schools will hire you to teach their employees how to use new gadgets and new software.

SUPPLIES

You will need advertising and your own up-to-date electronics at home on which to practice.

TIME NEEDED

When customers call—these customers likely won't be comfortable with talking online so you do need to make sure you are available by phone!—they tell you what they need to learn, and you decide how many hours the lessons will take. Plan a three-hour session for those who know nothing about their device. If people call for program or software lessons, allow two hours for the session.

WHAT TO CHARGE

$15 per hour for individual lessons. If you teach a group of people, such as employees of a company or school, charge a discounted rate per hour per individual, or negotiate a flat fee.

HOW TO ADVERTISE

Ask owners of local electronics stores to give your flyers to customers when they purchase something. See if you can leave flyers on the front desks of these stores. To persuade owners to distribute your flyers, tell them you will mention their stores to your customers.

Your flyer might say: "Are you frustrated with complicated computer books? Do you dread wading through thick manuals? Call E. Z. Bytes at 123-4567 for inexpensive tutoring by a tech-smart kid."

Distribute the flyers to business owners in your area. They may hire you to teach their employees. This type of flyer might say: "Increase productivity in your business by having your employees become computer literate and learn new software programs. Call E. Z. Bytes, a tech-smart kid, at 123-4567 for inexpensive group tutoring."

These days, a lot of people are pretty comfortable with technology, but there are always those who aren't—could you teach a class at a senior center?—and there is always new software and programs that even the most savvy of people need help staying current with.

HINTS

* You will need sound knowledge of electronics and popular programs in order to run this business, including some old ones that might not be sold much but are still widely used. You'll also need to stay on the bleeding edge—one step further than the cutting edge—to be prepared for tomorrow's new products. To get more information, read books at your local library, take classes at school, and subscribe to computer magazines—and, of course, research online and practice with actual computers, phones, e-readers, and programs! Learn how to use the most popular ones.

* When customers call you for help with something you don't know well, learn it quickly! Set up the tutoring appointment well in the future so you have enough time to learn. If you become familiar with many, you won't often encounter this situation.

* Teaching is difficult, and not all students catch on quickly. Be patient! And be patient with the technician, too.

INSPIRATION FROM KID ENTREPRENEURS JUST LIKE YOU!

NAME: The Depot Coffee House

TITLE: old train depot renovated into a coffee house, youth community project, and bike path trailhead

AGE: forever young

WHERE: Minnesota, USA

WHAT: The organic and fair-trade coffee flows each and every day and evening at the Depot, which is open to the public but focused on kids. There's a weekly open mic and high school bands book the Friday night live-music slots.

HOW: Wanting a fun drug-and-alcohol-free place to hang out, teens in suburban Minneapolis planned and opened the Depot in 1998, and it continues to be governed by a board made up of thirteen students and three adults. The local parks and school systems actively support the Depot, and the business is a learning lab for the school district's business department, meaning students have earned school credit by, for example, developing marketing plans that the Depot actually uses.

FUN FACT: The Depot became a Peace Site (www.peacesites.org) in 2003.

RESOURCE: www.thedepotcoffeehouse.com

53

Wake-Up Caller

The early bird gets the worm!

You call people at a prearranged time in the morning to wake them up. When you call, you say more than "Good morning!" or "Beep! Beep! Beep!" You give the date, a quick summary of the top news stories of the day, and the weather forecast for your area.

SUPPLIES

You will need your own alarm, a phone, and a newspaper subscription or internet connection.

TIME NEEDED

You need to be an early riser. Set aside thirty minutes in the morning to read the news carefully. Plan on spending another fifteen minutes summarizing the news and weather in a script for yourself. When you call customers, each call should last no longer than a minute.

WHAT TO CHARGE

$20 per month. Collect your fee at the beginning of the month, before you provide the service.

HOW TO ADVERTISE

Distribute flyers in your area. Your message might say: "Have trouble waking up in the morning? Hate the sound of an alarm? An early-rising, reliable kid will call you at a specified time and wake you up with a report of the day's news and weather. Call Vera Early at 123-4567 or email Vera@email.com to subscribe to this excellent service."

Don't hesitate to go door-to-door. When you meet people, explain how pleasant and informative it will be to wake up to the day's news and weather stories.

When customers call, agree upon a time when you will call each morning. Ask if they want weekend service. Have customers send a check for the first month's fee. If the customer is hesitant, offer to make one free wake-up call to prove the value of your service.

HINTS

* If you call a customer one morning, and that person reports that she is staying home sick, offer a polite wish that she feel better soon, ask if you should call the next day, if you're scheduled to, and get off the phone as quickly as possible so your client can get back to resting. The next time you call, ask how she's doing, or if the illness is major or prolonged, deliver a get-well-soon card or balloon.

* Some potential clients may say they don't need your service because they wake up to a radio alarm that is set right at the time the station is reading the news and weather. In those cases, offer something a little different. If the person likes poetry, you could read a short poem as your wake-up call. Or do a word-a-day wake-up call, and using the dictionary, teach your client an interesting new word each day.

INSPIRATION FROM KID ENTREPRENEURS JUST LIKE YOU!

NAME: Dino Zaharakis

TITLE: inventor, business founder

AGE: 11

WHERE: Pennsylvania, USA

WHAT: Dino is the founder of ZLabs, Inc., which invented One, a dock for a wide variety of electronic devices, from e-readers to tablets to phones.

HOW: As often happens with good ideas, Dino's dzdock came about because of a dare—and, of course, some entrepreneurial spirit. Dino's dad challenged him to create a great iPad dock—and promised to reward Dino with a phone of his own. After a lot of thought and play, making prototypes of his designs out of paper and aluminum, and working with local manufacturing companies, Dino got a whole lot more than just a new phone. Because ZLabs, Inc., works with local businesses as much as possible, Dino's whole community benefits, too.

FUN FACT: Dino plays lacrosse and customizes lacrosse sticks.

RESOURCE: www.dzdock.com

54

Website Designer

*Build websites,
build your future!*

You use your technology and art skills to create beautiful, functional websites for people who don't have the ability or time to do so.

SUPPLIES

You'll need a dedicated computer and a reliable internet connection that you can access at any time.

TIME NEEDED

In addition to advertising and selling your service, your time will be spent on building a website. Plan to meet with your client for thirty to sixty minutes to understand their website needs. It may take a couple of rounds of work to produce the final product—you'll prepare a draft website and show it to the client, the client will make suggestions, and you'll prepare another version of the site. Using the simplest site—a free blogging service that has pre-designed templates—may take you an hour. Fully designing and coding a website will take many more hours.

WHAT TO CHARGE

$25 per hour. Some customers may be interested in a flat project fee, so try to estimate ahead of time how many hours you'll work.

HOW TO ADVERTISE

The best advertisements for a website business are great websites! Your own and others that you've worked on. Show potential clients those.

Search online to see if each business in your neighborhood or town has a website. Call or visit those that don't and talk to them about how you can increase their sales by building them a beautiful and functional website.

Research what area school and non-school clubs, organizations, and teams don't have websites and meet with them about helping them grow their membership through a website designed by you.

HINTS

* Some businesses don't have websites because they don't know what makes a good website or how one will help their business. Consider that first meeting a teaching moment, too—help the customers understand what they need and want.
* Other businesses don't have the time or interest to maintain one. The information on a website must always be current, or people won't visit it. Consider offering web hosting, content maintenance, and tech support as additional services.
* Most businesses will want customers to be able to buy their products from their website, learn about events from an updated calendar, and contact the store through an online form. Clubs may want a special form for people interested in volunteering with or joining them. Even if you are building basic websites, you should probably know the options available for these services and be able to offer them. Customers who don't have much time or tech skill will need simple interactive features on their websites.

55

Window Washer

Dirty panes means business gains!

People hate looking through dirty windows. You make their windows sparkling clean. Homes and businesses will use your services.

SUPPLIES

You will need a phone or computer, window cleaner, flyers, and a rubber window wiper, microfiber cloths, or newspaper.

TIME NEEDED

To clean the inside and outside of windows will take about five hours for most houses. You can buy window cleaner, but you can also make your own inexpensively with water and vinegar or dish soap. Make a big batch at one time and transfer small amounts into spray bottles or buckets to take with you to a job. Look online for recipes—one of the keys to less streaking is to use less soap than you think you should.

WHAT TO CHARGE

$2 per window. Remind the customer that your price includes cleaning both sides of the window. If the customer wants only outside work done, charge $1.75 per window.

HOW TO ADVERTISE

Distribute flyers in your area. Your flyer might say: "Tired of looking through dirty windows? Hate to see the world in a haze? Let an industrious kid scrub your windows until they're sparkling clean. Call C. D. Light at 123-4567 or email CD@email.com for the cheapest rates in town."

Knock on doors and carry a small piece of clean, shiny glass. You might say to potential customers: "I can make your windows this clean! Wouldn't you rather hire me than spend your weekend washing windows? If you already have a person washing your windows, I'll bet my prices are less." If the homeowner is unsure, offer to wash one window for free. If the person agrees to have you wash the windows, make an appointment to return and do the work.

Businesses will need their windows washed. Visit local store owners and describe your service. If possible, arrange to visit the business every month to wash the windows.

HINTS

* If you can please a client on the first visit, you will be called every time the windows get dirty. After getting paid for your work, be sure to give the client five flyers to keep and to pass on to friends.
* Though you can use old rags or paper towels to dry windows, those often leave streaks or lint. Use microfiber cloths or newspaper instead.
* When cleaning windows in summer, you'll get thirsty. Bring a container of water and don't ask the customer for a drink. Bring a snack, too, if you're going to be out all day.

Window Washer

* If a client asks you to climb a ladder or to go out on a balcony to wash a window, say you can't. Tell the client you're happy to wash the other windows, but you're not allowed to do anything dangerous. You may also need to ask your customer to help you remove and then replace screens. You don't want to accidentally damage them.
* You may want to bring some music, but be sure to use head-phones. Keep your music quiet so you can hear if the client calls you.
* If you run this enterprise, you'll look forward to storms. They'll be your business partner by making windows dirty!

Resources

For further guidance, check out the following websites and links. Information changes all the time, so you should research whatever is most common, most approved, and most appropriate for you and your business right now.

NEWS, FEATURES, CONFERENCES

* www.angel.co
* www.juniorbiz.com
* https://www.disability.gov/home/i_want_to/self-employment/resources_for_young_entrepreneurs
* http://nni.arizona.edu/nayec/index.php

CHILD LABOR LAWS

* http://www.dol.gov/whd/childlabor.htm
* http://www.youthrules.dol.gov/index.htm

ONLINE FUND-RAISING

* www.kickstarter.com
* www.indiegogo.com
* www.invested.in

WEBSITE AND SOCIAL MEDIA RESOURCES

* www.wordpress.com
* www.blogger.com
* www.linkedin.com
* www.twitter.com
* www.facebook.com
* www.youtube.com
* www.plus.google.com

VIRTUAL MARKETS

* www.ebay.com
* www.craigslist.org
* www.etsy.com

About the Author

THEN

When Daryl Bernstein first published *Better Than a Lemonade Stand!*, he was a fifteen-year-old honors student from Scottsdale, Arizona. At age eight, he started his first business. He went to school one day wanting to buy books at a school fair, but his parents had forgotten to give him money. Daryl decided to earn his own in the hours before the fair. He created a highly profitable business manufacturing and selling small paper toys, and within an hour, the fad caught on and every student wanted one. By the time the fair started, Daryl had earned enough money to purchase more books than anyone! He has been running his own businesses ever since.

At the time he wrote this book, Daryl owned a successful graphic design company. He used his computer to create custom logos and flyers for small businesses. He also ran a house-checking service that was both fun and profitable. In his free time, Daryl played tennis and baseball, attended spring training baseball games, and worked on writing projects—like this book.

Daryl also enjoyed investing his earnings in the stock, bond, and options markets. This interest paid off when Daryl won the regional and state competitions of National History Day and flew to Washington, DC, to compete in the nationals. His project was titled *Big Blue*, and it detailed the relationship between the fluctuations in IBM's stock price and IBM's technological advances. And what did Daryl read for fun? *The Wall Street Journal*, of course!

NOW

Today, Daryl Bernstein is still an entrepreneur, and he's also a technology investor and speaker. He is founder and CEO of RightSignature, a popular software service for getting documents signed online with handwritten signatures. With a user base of both small businesses and enterprises, RightSignature.com enables parties to fill out and sign contracts, forms, and other business-critical documents in any web browser or on a mobile device.

Daryl was also the founder of Global Video, a market-leading educational media distributor and producer, which was acquired by School Specialty (Nasdaq: SCHS). He is an advisor to and investor in innovative software-as-a-service companies, including MindBody and YouMail.

A sought-after speaker, Daryl has been featured in media around the world, including CNN, CBS, NPR, Radio 3 Hong Kong, *The Wall Street Journal*, *The Los Angeles Times*, El Mundo, and TechCrunch. He is also the author of *The Venture Adventure* (Atria Books/Beyond Words), was named a Global Leader for Tomorrow by the World Economic Forum, and was featured in *Chicken Soup for the Entrepreneur's Soul* (HCI).

Learn more at www.darylbernstein.com.